Buttonwood Cottage

Buttonwood Cottage

Rue Matthiessen

ISBN: 978-0-9896124-2-5 (paperback)

978-0-9896124-1-8 (e-book)

FarrarFiles

For Steve

Contents

Acknowledgments

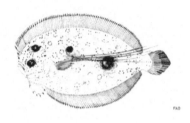

This book began as a Blog. My many thanks to early readers who became faithful enthusiasts. Among them Maria Matthiessen, Steve Shaughnessy, Alex Matthiessen, Dorothy Sherry, Sylvia Sherry, Linda Sherry, Lisbet Rogers, Mary Lehmann, Nathalie Love, Suzanne McNear, Laura Meiselman, Sarah Koenig, Eileen Grigg, Stuart Lowrie, Ken Dorph, Blair Seagram, Cecil Bazelon, Jessie Pollock, Johanna Maria Van Rooij and Posy Abbot. A special thanks to Maria Matthiessen for her helpful editing suggestions, Steve Shaughnessy for his eagle eye, and to Blair Seagram for help with the layout and design. And to Michele McManus, who has accompanied many snorkel expeditions on Bonaire.

My gratitude as well to Captain Don and Janet Thibault for excerpts from "Reef Windows," for the early pictures of Don and the Valerie Queen. And to Alex Dzierba, for beautiful photos underwater and above, featured in this book. Also, many thanks to Greenlabel, the landscapers who have taken care of our garden all along, and neighbors Yvonne Domecasse and Benjamin Machenna from across the street, and to Hans Reitveld, who directed our renovation.

Biography

Rue Matthiessen is based in New York City and the East End of Long Island. She was a reporter for *the East Hampton Star*, and has been published in many literary journals. In 2017, an essay, "Real Life," was nominated for the Pushcart Prize. This is her first independently published work.

Bonaire, April

Monday

Got a direct flight, seated among a very loud, obnoxious group of American divers, one of whom couldn't seem to withstand two seconds of silence while awake . . . Between the divers and the late-night flight and my nervousness about having gotten into a contract on a house that I haven't been inside of, on an island I've been to only once, and that my husband, Steve, has not been to at all—I got very little sleep. Landing at 4:30 a.m., I deplaned in the dark, the lovely, soft breeze of the leeward Antilles on my face.

First, of course, I drove to Kaya India, the street where the house is. By the time I arrived, the dawn had cast a cement-colored pall, and what was a pretty street with little houses seemed to have no charm at all. There was also a scary looking brown and black pig in the yard, and chickens and roosters on the road. A house that I had liked so much the last time, on an adjoining street, Kaya Serena, was FOR SALE, at which point I truly wondered what it was I had gotten myself into.

I should preface this by saying that Kaya India #8 wasn't for sale when I first saw it. My real estate agent on Bonaire, Anja Romeijnders, had been driving me around and only happened to pass by it. I asked her to stop and go back. It was rundown, so much that I thought it might be abandoned, but then I saw a couple of kids playing in the dirt yard. The yard was a big, appealing square; the house was a simple one-story bungalow with good proportions. I took a picture. Once back in New York, I couldn't get that little house out of my mind.

Anja hadn't show me anything else I liked in our price range. I've worked in real estate and know that one can easily find an owner and make an offer.

From New York, over about two weeks, we negotiated with the owners through the agency, and settled on a number.

Back to the pig and the dawn. All the houses were shabbier than I remembered—paint peeling, wilted-looking kitchen gardens in pots. I drove up and down as quietly and stealthily as I could so as not to wake anyone, wondering—what have I done? I circled the block of streets—Kaya Serena, Kaya Antonio Newman, Kaya America—noticing a few lights flicking on as people got up early for work. I drove off to the Caribbean Club where I had a room, but couldn't get in because check-in wasn't until 3:00 p.m. So I parked in front and stretched on the backseat, bandanna on my eyes thinking—WHAT HAVE I DONE? I couldn't sleep of course, so I drove all the way back to Kaya

India again. On second look, the birds were beginning their morning riot, and there were many, and the scary pig was gone. I saw our house from the back view (from Kaya Mississippi), and noticed how the plot of land *was* really nice and big, just asking for a tropical garden. The houses in the neighborhood were a little shabby but loved. This house, our house, was neglected, but again I could see its potential to be a cheerful place. I also found, around the corner, on Kaya America, the Lizard Inn. There were lots of cars in front of it, the kind that vacationers and divers rent. Thinking *if they can do it, I can do it*, I felt better. Chances were good that we might get income of some kind, and it would be okay if we didn't spend a fortune on renovations. And that we would love coming here when we can. Because it's so beautiful.

I later went down to the sea (so close, so lovely) and had a few espressos and an overpriced sandwich at a restaurant overlooking the water. A small finch-like bird, (a bananaquit), hopped onto the table and cocked his head at me before darting in for the sugar. Indeed all around me at that early hour were the tweets and shrieks and hoots and howls of Bonaire's avian population. I decided I'd get a bird guide, so I could learn what they are called. My heart was so lifted by this little fellow. It seemed as if he was there to remind me of what had compelled me to do this nutty thing in the first place—the bird and sea life of Bonaire, still so much in evidence everywhere here.

Tuesday

Whereas Kaya India is only a drive of a few minutes from Kralendijk, the Caribbean Club is quite a ways out of the town. Miles and miles of undeveloped land surround the place, and beyond that, the Washington Slagbaai park. It is the first and only national park in the entire leeward Antilles, and has some 5.643 hectares. By getting up early I was able to identify, on the edge of this open land, trupials, bananaquits, Caribbean mocking birds, wild parrots and parakeets, and last but not least, an emerald hummingbird.

I had never seen the inside of the house, and couldn't get until Thursday, when I had an appointment with the owner, Javier Sof. Also, real estate agent Anja and technical inspector Hans Rietveld would be there. So I had a little time to kill before that. In my rental car I drove past Kaya India maybe five times, checking out the comings and goings of the neighbors, and how it looked at different times of the day.

A little later, while walking in Kralendijk, I thought I heard church singing, and followed the sound to the sea. I found a beautiful little open-air chapel overlooking the water; all the windows and doors open. I fell into step with another late arrival, a woman in a hat and Sunday finery. We stood in the big, open door, listening to the Dutch choir, and the service which was in Papiamento and Dutch. Someone got some folding chairs so we could sit, and we shared a program. Singing in Papiamento was easy, though the Dutch was hard to read, and she was very out of tune. I had to listen hard to the in-tune singer on my left in order not to go off track. Her name was Juliana, and she was pointing to prayers (one looked like the Lord's Prayer in Papiamento). She wanted to commiserate with me on the goodness of the Lord. Which was very sweet. I felt like a fraud with my camera, sneaking pictures of the congregation. It was children's day at the chapel, so at the end, the children came up to the front, all in their Sunday best. I have heard that this is a very Catholic country.

Wednesday

At the Caribbean Club I had a nice outdoor area to sit in, private with a few chairs barricaded around from prying eyes. Here I meditated in the mornings and tried not to think too much. With more than a day more to wait before getting into the house on Kaya India, I was very curious! I went to the dive shop at the resort, looking for a "dive buddy," because one should never dive alone. It would be stupid. I recently got my license in February, on Bonaire, on my first trip here when I took the picture of the house. I have about nine dives under my belt. At the dive shop they put me with Marie, a tall Dutch girl a little younger than me, who speaks very good English. She has about 40 dives, but she has always gone with a couple of friends from Holland, who are much more experienced than she is. This was the first time that she would be the leader, she said. She emphasized that we do everything very slowly, and take our time, which was certainly okay with me. This would be the first time I was going without an instructor.

We agreed on a 40-minute dive, heading against the current first, going no more than 60 feet down, doing a safely stop at 20 feet, and returning with at least 1,000 "bar" of air left in our tank, in order not to cut it too close. We got outfitted with the equipment and drove over to Captain Don's Habitat, a small resort founded by an American named Don Stewart. His discovery of the reef in the mid-sixties was the start of the dive culture particular to Bonaire, called "diving freedom." It meant that people with only an open water license, like Marie and I, could rent equipment and dive anywhere they want, without expensive boats and chaperones.

While we were getting set on the dock, I noticed that Marie was hyperventilating and I was nervous too, teeth chattering in the sun. There is always something one has to get over before strapping on all of this gear and plunging into the depths of the sea. I can't imagine ever feeling very relaxed about it. The reward comes just at the moment one plunges in and is suddenly weightless. It feels so natural that the other danger is to really believe that one is a fish and become over confident about the equipment . . . which was not going to be my problem today, or ever again.

We went in. I should say that sometimes my favorite part of a dive is in the shallows at 10-15 feet, on a sunny day, because the sun slices down through the water (warmer than the deeps), and bounces back from the white coral sand, illuminating everything. On this day, there was a school of silvery fish with yellow stripes hovering between the dock pilings, and queen parrotfish and French angelfish darting here and there. I also like the shallows because there isn't really far to go between the bottom and my own natural habitat above the water.

We gave each other the "okay" sign and headed out to greater depths to the drop off, where the reef plummets to the sea floor. One has to get on the edge of it and work down, trusting oneself to the abyss. Fortunately, there's a lot to look at on the reef wall—a phantasmagoria of darker corals, and innumerable varieties of colorful fish, some single, some big, and some smaller and some tiny, glassy ghosts of the bigger fish they would soon be, swimming in perfect, musical patterns.

I was on the reef side, with Marie to my left, swimming a few feet ahead. She turned around occasionally to point out something and give the "okay" sign. And for a while, everything went well. Then, about 15 minutes along, I started to feel this clanking and rattling in the area of my tank, on my back, and reached back to find, to my horror, that the tank had slid down in the holder, just about sliding off, which would take the regulator and the mouthpiece out of my mouth, leaving me to drown. There's nothing quite like the purity of this kind of terror. Twisting around, I grabbed for the bottom of the tank, which I managed to hook with my fingers, all while trying to keep up with Marie, screaming for her attention and not getting it. Marie had that "fish feeling," and was zooming along, having forgotten about me and everything else for a few moments. These moments to me were eons and eons, but to anyone else, including Marie, probably just about 40 seconds. I was panicking, trying to hold on to the tank and the regulator in my mouth, yelling, gesticulating, wondering whether I should ditch Marie and bolt for the surface (about 40 feet up), or just turn right to get to the shallows while still underwater. Acutely miserable, my heart exploding out of my chest, I began to wonder if my life was just going to end, 40 feet under the sea, thousands of miles from home, with a child still to raise. Was that going to be it? How stupid, was all I could think. And truly, the thought did occur, that all of this Bonaire stuff was just a mid-life crisis thing, a last crazy blast before I slowly start to sink into the ground. All my workouts at the gym, my vain, pointless efforts to stay young and not turn completely into a hausfrau, along with some ridiculous notion of an international, adventure-filled existence with a Stan Getz soundtrack had gotten me into this predicament, 35 goddamn feet under the ocean, and it was finally just going to end it for me, and create a huge, stupid deficit in the lives of the people I love. Emmett motherless, Steve a widower. Back home they would all shake their heads, the more cautious among them remaking the story of my demise into a cautionary fable. Out in a blaze of the ridiculous and the desperate, not to mention the quotidian. In between underwater screams, I pondered these options for milliseconds, and remembered learning in dive school that mostly everything can be fixed under the water. I chose not to bolt; I could still breathe and scream through the regulator. While holding onto this trailing tank, I stopped trying to catch her. Miraculously, at the moment I gave up, she turned around to check on me. She grabbed the tank and basically shook me up and down like a party favor until the tank was re-positioned, tightened the strap, and we went on, finishing the dive. She never knew, until I told her, how frightened I had been. Later on, over Margaritas, she complimented me for "not panicking."

Thursday

Went to Sunbelt Realty first thing to arrange all the appointments with the contractors later in the week, and to confirm that I'd be meeting owner Javier at 2:00 p.m. to finally see the inside of the house. Because my cell phone costs about $5 every time I turn it on, I have to do everything the old-fashioned way, (very old-fashioned), as if the phone itself has yet to be invented. That is because people assume I *have* a cell phone, and don't offer access to their landlines. And if I don't get back right away, because I can't, they assume I'm nonfunctioning, nonexistent, or not serious. Anja wasn't at the office but I spoke with her associate, Martijn, and asked for some architect's names. He made a few calls and set up an appointment for me to meet with a guy on Kaya Industria at 10:00. The other two didn't answer, which I'm finding to be a sort of pattern on Bonaire—people are not completely invested in the idea of work. If they happen to fall into it, fine. And if work is unable to catch up with them, they will find something else to do with their time.

The technical inspector, Hans, had made a little drawing of the house that I took with me to see the architect. The architect, a big tall blond Dutch guy (they are like Amazons), was a bit intimidating in his sleek, modern office, all gleaming white surfaces and floor-to-ceiling windows. He had a sidekick, a sort of apprentice, also an Amazon, only with dark hair. We all sat down in the conference room, around this huge oval table, which immediately dwarfed my drawing, my house, and my existence. I wondered, as we got into it, if I was just an opportunity for the architect to practice his English.

He got out a sheet of vellum and laid it over the drawing, speaking rapidly as he made a few sketches of different possibilities, raising the roof six to ten feet, with terracotta tiles on the new roof, extending the porch around the west and north side of the house where the kitchen was, and also where the land is biggest. This, along with the raised roof, would make the house cooler and more spacious. He enlarged the windows and added more windows all along the new porch, which would be another living area, with ceiling fans and a little bar area. I might even have a little walkway to another building, say, a guesthouse? A studio for Steve? They were great suggestions, fabulous suggestions—the prospect of turning this shack into some sort of plantation-style, Palm Beach cottage—centered around the idea of living outdoors and drinking more wine than I should, and being lulled to sleep on my terracotta porch by the whir of the fans and the sheltering whisper of the palm trees we would also put in—was so delicious it rolled around on my tongue. Until we got to the cost.

Bonaire is more remote than its sister islands of Aruba and Curacao, in part because it is comparatively underpopulated. Because there are only about 17,000 people, shipments are few and far between, and all building materials must, of course, arrive by boat. A termite problem (called white ants), narrows the choices one has. Almost all of the construction is rebar (iron rods) and cinder block, with concrete poured in for stability. I know this also because on the island there are a number of half-finished houses like abandoned Lego projects, with stacks of blocks with the rebar sticking out. When I asked Anja about it, she said that some were aborted projects from the 2008 downturn. Costs of materials seem to be commensurate with their weight, made worse by the price of oil. In the U.S., putting up a cinder block structure would be one of the cheapest ways to build a house, with a wooden structure being quite a lot more expensive. Here, it's the reverse.

That is why, back at the architect's office, I found out that to raise the roof and put on a decent-sized porch would cost at least $100,000, without even adding a bedroom or a bathroom. I tried to remain businesslike and not show how crestfallen I felt. I had the same sinking feeling as I did after I'd gotten off the plane and driven by the house. The most miserable, sick, sinking feeling that I have squandered this money, like people who actually *buy* houses or land sight unseen, (in the desert for example, at $75 per acre), or in foreign countries or just places that they are unfamiliar with, or about as familiar with as I was with Bonaire. I'd explained to Marie over dinner the night before that I had researched Bonaire, but frankly, this whole thing had been mostly out of a feeling, an inkling, that so many elements are right, and that the time is right, and why not do this now, because if I don't do it now I might never do it, and I've thought about owning a house in the Caribbean for a long time. That is not a cool-headed sort of decision; that's a soul decision and that's how people get into trouble. I have been impulsive in my life, and tend to move very quickly when I want something, and I have been lucky a lot of the time that things have just worked out. I couldn't help but seriously fear that again I had made a big mistake, that it was just too crazy this time.

As I sat there shaking my head at these numbers, I could see that the architect and his sidekick felt sorry for me. But not too sorry to venture, delicately, the question that was clearly hanging in the air, if a business relationship were to proceed. How much did we pay for the house?

$105,000, I said. The Amazon collapsed a bit in his chair, deflating slowly with sympathy. *Why did I?* he asked. *Because that's what it took,* I said. And I added that the technical inspector said the house was sound, and we could renovate for $30,000. The two looked at each other, as if to seriously question the quality of such a renovation.

Then he perked up in that socially deft way that Europeans have, that for all of its skill is somehow not shallow, and said, "Well! This is just one opinion, see what the others say." He saw the situation, saw it whole, and with a nice sort of clarity, wished me luck.

At 2:00 p.m. that same day, agent Anja, inspector Hans, and owner Javier, met me at Kaya India for the tour.

Javier greeted me at the door with a big smile, as did Anja and Hans. The fragility in their smiles included the knowledge that this was my first time inside the house, and that there was no backing out of the signed contract without me forfeiting a hefty wad of cash. I was still vibrating from the interview with the architect and feeling quite desperate for the news that this renovation could somehow be achieved for the numbers stated by Hans in the report.

So, in I went through the front sliding door, the three of them in the periphery of my vision like school teachers on test day. A few tattered arm chairs on the right, long rectangular living space, a high, square kitchen table with a plastic tablecloth, a window looking over the north side of the property. A kitchen with a gas bottle on the floor, a rickety, grease-stained kitchen block, an outsized refrigerator, and an oven. Javier had cleaned the place up somewhat since the pictures were taken by Hans and sent to me in New York. To the left, two thirds of the way back, the bathroom, (decent sized, ugly tiles), and on either side—the back bedroom (painted purple) and the front bedroom (yellow with a built-in closet). Back to the living room/kitchen area, where the kitchen door to the left of the stove led out to the spacious, deep backyard, with 50 percent more land, in fact, than we have in Sag Harbor. Mostly dirt, with some sparse grass and an overgrowth of brush over the makeshift cesspool, (called a beer-put), on the south side of the house. No dividing wall between the property and the neighbor to the back. Javier mentioned that they might chip in for a new wall. The neighbor's orange house was clearly visible, as was the two-story concrete house overlooking the north side of the property, in fact, looking *into* the property in a disconcerting way. The dividing walls on the north and south sides were mostly bare, graced with an aborted painting project in one spot, graffiti in another, and hardened cement oozing out between the cinder block. At the front of the property were four gorgeous trees. The prettiest of the four had a sofa parked underneath it.

Javier was much younger than I had expected, a shy, sweet sort of guy, born on Bonaire in 1984. He explained that he had owned the house for two years, and that he bought it from his parents. In Bonaire, there is a provision in the law called "Island Territories." It allows native citizens of Bonaire to claim land for a nominal fee, if they build on it. I gathered that his parents had claimed the land and built the house in 1990, though they couldn't keep it up, so they had sold it to him. In residence with him now were his mother, his sister, and her children. After this, they would stay on the island, though he didn't say where and I didn't pry.

Though there was not one thing to steal, he didn't allow us at any time over the next few days to be in the house without him. In the end, I interviewed three different contractors, going through and getting ideas from all, getting a feel for them and whom I might work with best. During all of this, Javier was listening keenly, helping out with suggestions here and there. I have been through three renovations (an upstairs apartment, a downstairs apartment, and a studio) in Sag Harbor, two of which I general contracted, and also did the interior design. The last one was so stressful that I got shingles at the end.

But as a result, I wasn't completely at a loss with the contractors on Bonaire, mostly understanding what they were saying, and taking notes all the way through. The first thing would be to get rid of the concrete porch in the front. It could be demolished and carted away for not much money, said Hans, because on Bonaire, there's a big dump somewhere and garbage is not really regulated. We both commented that this was a shame, though for me, at that moment, would save quite a lot. The demolition and carting part of a project on Long Island is very costly. Another guy suggested that while we were replacing the soft board ceiling of the purple bedroom, it would be a good idea to make an entrance to the underside of the roof in case animals like iguanas got in.

Hans, who was a perceptive fellow, was as helpful as he could be, while gently easing me into the idea of scaling down my plans, forgetting about adding beds and baths and covered porches. He let me babble away . . .

Nice layout, we wouldn't need a lot of house or a lot of room, would we? It's really about being outside . . . If we just restored what was here, it could still be quite nice for us, or as a rental for two couples or a small family? With landscaping to screen the neighbor out . . . Could we do it at around 30k? Really?

Yes, he said, in the flesh, which is different than looking at something as an attachment in an e-mail. As per his estimate, he said that we would have to have all new burglary-proof windows and doors, because of the petty theft problem on the island. We would need that especially if we wanted to do a dive vacation rental. One of the other contractors I spoke to, a young American guy, (born on Bonaire), who was recommended to me said, "You have to really be aware of the theft problem. Once it gets out that Americans (us) have redone the house, they'll be onto you fast." Despite his youth, he had an air of being the old sage of Bonaire. He recommended raising the walls around the property and installing a gate with a lock. And then, out of the blue, he said, "You don't really like America that much anymore, do you?" I could only answer that with a smile, because the real answer was way too complicated.

The house did seem solid to me, only minor cracks in the walls that could be repaired with plaster. According to Hans, the wiring in the walls had been tested, and would handle the upgraded electricity and additional outlets that would have to be installed. Besides the bathroom, there were three more different tile colors on the floors. Instead of taking all of these out, Hans thought we should just put new, lighter tile over it to create continuity between the living area and bedrooms, making the place look brighter and larger. The bathroom would stay the same, in order to keep costs down. A shower heater, a new shower fixture. A good scrub. A factory kitchen, ordered from the local supplier, Kooyman. A new refrigerator and an enclosure outside the back kitchen door, for a washing machine and a gas bottle. Other steps would be to take one window out of the living room to create more passive space, and changing the front slider to a window, and adding a new sliding door on the side of the house. In Bonaire, it's all about the trade winds, because they are so pleasant and help the house stay cool. With a sliding door on the side and the new window, and enlarging the two kitchen windows and making the back door "all shutters," we would maximize the east-west breeze through the house. Because of the cost of electricity, most places I have stayed have air-conditioning only in the bedrooms, which is used only at night. Which was fine with me, because I can't stand it. Then I remembered what Steve was most concerned about, and what I would want too—an outdoor space of some kind, shaded from the sun.

Hans and I then went around to the north side of the property, where there was the most space. He thought that for not too much money we could put in a concrete porch, three meters wide, running the length of the living room side of the house. What about shade? He suggested a wooden trellis over it, with plants growing up and over, and additional landscaping for privacy and shade. This way, he said, we'd avoid having to get permits, (time-consuming and expensive), because such a structure was not considered an extension. Also, no permits to move doors and windows around, another plus. He said he would make a drawing and send it to me. At this point, I started feeling better about the whole thing. The night before at the Caribbean Club, I had looked up into the 15-foot-high ceiling. Though it certainly felt airy, I noticed that there was a leak and a water stain. We already have a big house in Sag Harbor and a lot to take care of. Why would we need more? Here it was all about the sea, the reef, the people, and the birds.

And despite that the owners had let it get rundown, there was a cheerful feeling in the house. I felt that Javier and his family had been happy here, and it was also good for them to move on. Before he left, Javier asked me to contact him when the project was done so he could come over and see it, and I said I would. I met the neighbor across the street, Yvonne Domacasse. She had noticed me driving by numerous times in the rental truck. She was very friendly, and promised to "keep a look out," on the place. The neighbor with the two-story house overlooking our plot drove off, and I could see by the lettering on his truck that he worked for STINAPA, the national park of Bonaire. Another positive thing.

Later in the afternoon, Hans took me around to look at some projects he had worked on, and also his own house, a nice place in a similar neighborhood, crammed with books and surrounded with native trees, bushes, and plants, many flowering. He said he had hummingbirds there. Because his style was so different, I mentioned the white gravel I'd seen in a lot of places, which gets dirty and has a lot of glare, with baby palm trees plunked down here and there. He said he hated the look of the white gravel, and that it was hot besides. He suggested that I go with native tamarinds, sea grapes and chinkswood trees, with leafy paths leading through, like he had done. Plant to dispel the heat and encourage wildlife. I walked around, taking pictures, and relaxed a little more, while he printed out the TV station list from Telbo, the cable and internet provider on the island. By the next day, I decided to hire Hans for the job, as he seemed to be the most knowledgeable and clearheaded, understanding my vision and budget. But the thing that really sealed it for me was the hummingbirds. It would be hard not to trust someone who cared about hummingbirds, and I knew Steve would feel the same.

Friday

I went for one more dive, before leaving Bonaire and returning to New York, to begin the long-distance renovation of Kaya India.

I played Joao Donato's "Muito a Vontade" through my computer, to keep things light, while packing sun block, snacks, water, and calling up the front desk to reserve the equipment. In the diving world, they often say that it's better to have your own equipment that you are familiar with. This, I can really understand. I imagined buying it in the future and storing it somewhere on the island, or even taking it around the world to different destinations. Though, with now having to pay for checked luggage, that could be very expensive, and I always have computers and cameras too that have to come in the cabin. My Dutch friends left their computers back at their jobs, where they probably belong, and Marie has her own diving equipment. On KLM, the main airline from the Netherlands, they check the dive gear for free, though the few airlines that come here from the U.S. charge for every last toothpick. They also have only one flight a week from the east coast (Newark), and one per week from Atlanta, while KLM flies at least once a day, twice the distance, for half the price. If one isn't lucky enough to get on the one flight from the U.S., a trip that should be four and a half hours can take all day with connecting flights. The first time, I went through Bogota and then Curacao. I've heard quite a few Americans complaining about it, while at the same time loving Bonaire's remoteness and rural quality. For me, the value of an experience seems to be in direct proportion to its rarity, its strangeness. If a place is easy, the focus is fuzzy, the senses less alert to the surroundings. The sacred hours that one has set aside as restorative are not, because one has switched locales, but not mentalities.

There are gated communities here and condo complexes that are owned mostly by Americans. The expenses of these investment/rental properties are covered by the income from dive rentals that they generate, giving the owners a place to perch in the winter months that looks pretty much like Florida. I know, because I looked at them. In all honesty, I sometimes envy the safety of such an investment, while knowing that we are priced out of those, and that we really wouldn't want them anyway. I know lots of people on Long Island who drive the best cars and live in perfect houses, have stable jobs, environments that are safe and predictable, and are insured to the hilt. They get all of this, and then they wonder why the color has drained from the scene.

Kaya India is in Playa Pabou (Pa-bow), a neighborhood that has many locals, and by that I mean people whose families have been on Bonaire for centuries. It isn't scrubbed clean, things are in transition. It's hard to say exactly how our house will turn out, in terms of fitting ourselves in. Suffice to say that we will *have* to fit ourselves in, and change and adapt, instead of buying where there are lots of people like us, in just another place with people who think just like we do.

The experience of diving is much the same. One is adapting to the environment or well . . . I was trying not to dwell on the alternative as we loaded up the truck. There is certainly a lot of *stuff*, a lot of it heavy. A tank that has approximately 45 minutes of air (depending on how fast you are breathing) weighs at least

30 pounds. I had jittery feelings again, and Marie did too—I could tell. The whole thing is not natural, not normal. You get stuck between your instincts, which are telling you to stay on shore, and your imagining of what you'd be missing just under the seductive and glittering surface of the water. You get prematurely jealous of the things other people who braved it will see that you will not see if you stay in your safe place. In the end you can't *not* do it. I thought about the many "professionals" who comprise the diving population, coming to Bonaire from all over the world. I've seen them in the bars and restaurants here. Very few sloppy drunks; in fact none.

You can't drink a lot and dive, unless you are suicidal. Instead, lots of straight white teeth, gradual tans, and trim waists and butts like soccer balls in rumpled but expensive linen clothes. People with massive jobs and impressive resumes (I don't count myself in this number), who have set aside their precious time to do this thing. On the drive over with Marie, (big job in the E.U.), I thought that all of these highly productive people can't be as nuts as I am—they are in fact doctors, lawyers, task-finishers, and top producers of every ilk, knowing what they were about by the age of 15, (I don't count myself in this number), and logically, how could the risk of early death-by-diving really be that high for them to do it again and again all day long here, sometimes three dives in a day, two in the day and one at night?

Marie and I drove about 20 minutes to what was just a parking area on the north side of the island, marked with a painted rock that said "Karpata." There was one other truck in the small parking area, and a long wooden staircase that ran down a cliff side to a coral beach. No ambulances, hospitals, or de-compression chambers in sight. Just wild, wild nature. A blue iguana, about seven inches long shimmied across the grey stones and gravel. Behind him, some scruffy bushes, the cliff drop, and the bands of blue ice, sapphire, and cobalt that define the sea around Bonaire. This was my first real "free dive." The last dive and all the others before were first in front of the dive shop in Kralendijk, and then at resorts where they have all the equipment and instructors on shore—not helpful in the least when 40 feet under the sea, but still nice to know.

A small concrete landing jutted out into the light chop. It took us at least 15 minutes to get sorted out and down the staircase, the iguana glancing at us now and then with his blue marble eyes. Needless to say, we took a lot of time over making sure my tank was secure. When we still weren't certain, we waited while a family (mother, father, and a girl about 15 years old) picked their way down the staircase, dragging all their gear, and Marie asked the dad, in Dutch, to help us. One of the stupidest things I had done the other time was forget to hook the fail-safe nylon strap over the neck of the tank, a mistake I'll never make again. We thanked them and, while holding onto the side of the pier, wobbled out over the slippery rocks into the shallows and into the drink.

Diving really is like leaving planet earth altogether, along with all of its problems.

On this day, along with the otherworldly feeling came a sense of happening into a giant party, a Studio 54-sized bash in the eighties without the noise. Though we had spent the entire morning trying to get to the party, having thoughts about it and preparing for it, we had been helpless to envision it from shore. The fish swam in interconnected webs, moving this way and that as if pulled by invisible strings, the way their egg-brethren do and have done since the beginning of time. They gave us wall-eyed looks, their dumb fish eyes barely registering us, which had the effect of including us as they wafted aside, bouncing nonchalantly in the wake, a lot like a late night crowd at a club when things have really taken off. The sea fans waved under the whoosh of our fins, bouncing to the invisible beat. A single Moray eel lurked under his/her rock, its toothy grin agape, darting back in as we passed. The eccentric of the bunch, he wants to be revered and feared but can't stand the glare of attention long enough to be frightening. The Christmas tree worm plucked its tentacles in as we passed—*no problem*, it seemed to say, ejecting its tentacles again, *this is just what I do, so you do what you do, everyone is accepted.*

Then we came to the drop off. At a 15-foot elevation, the reef below our fins disappeared. We drifted down the side of an underwater canyon, one of many that lie along the leeward coast. In order to avoid fatigue, we swam against the current first, though at 20 feet and below one hardly notices the current going in any one direction, because the entire picture sways gently left and right, up and down, bopping to the beat. Marie pointed out a pack of five permit fish, big brutes with domed heads looming on the cliff wall, their scales as shiny as polished coins. To crash the party and instantly be one of the gang is seductive. With the equipment you are in the club, breathing like a fish. The air in the tank provides a bit of a buzz, and it's easy to get carried away and forget that your element is not here, but somewhere above in the oxygenated, troubled world.

It was deliciously fun. Side by side, we wafted over the deep canyons, the sand chutes, the forests of gorgonians, elkhorn and fan coral. I tend to look at what's close to me, right in my field of vision—usually what is directly below. But Marie likes to look around and point things out. She signaled up and to the left and there was a hawksbill turtle, swimming not very fast. Its half-lidded eyes took in a scene we knew so little and it knew so well, its wing-like flippers keeping it in a steady forward motion, an entirely different movement than any kind of fish. Which made it a *presence*. An anomaly, a rarity. While the fish were darting hither and thither, the turtle radiated solemnity and ancient repose. I was later to read that all the big turtles of the sea are solitary creatures, traveling great distances in the world alone. Maybe that's why the mood of the party changed as it went through, from silly and cliquish and taken up with a lot of fanfare and frippery, to something deeper and more profound. We gaped at it as it slowly flew over the canyon and into the northerly distance, with the same steady whoosh of flipper, and all-knowing, irreverent, gaze. I gave Marie a thumbs up, the sign for everything from "I'm okay," to "Wow can you believe that?", which felt inadequate in the extreme. Later, on shore, we gushed about the dive and all that we saw, clambering up the stairs with all of the stuff. Marie had seen turtles before, but she was as thrilled as I was. On the drive home, we seized upon the moment to tell each other quirks of family and relationships and things hitherto not touched upon, all in a rush, safe in that ethereal window between Karpata and the topside world.

Sag Harbor, June & July

I have a certain sort of luck with houses. In college, I always landed the best dorm rooms, though it was purely by chance, because it was through a lottery system. The early boon of living, at 19, in a Tudor mansion with a view of the Catskill Mountains, and a semi-private bathroom with a Victorian tub (in which I hid for the first year), lifted the confusion and collapsed spirits that afflicted me at the time. The white tile, the quiet, the tear drop of rust in the sink from the faucet, the rumbles of old pipes in good repair deep within the bowels of the mansion, all were soothing, a structure that wouldn't let me down. I never asked the maintenance people if I could see the boiler room; I wish I had. Those high ceilings, walls of thick plaster, and stone terraces overlooking the mountains were the only things between me and desolation, though I wasn't yet curious about the way it all worked. I feel connected to houses, especially old ones, (our house in Sag Harbor was built in 1899). I am attuned to their sounds, their leaks and drips and creaks, their neglected corners, the odd hanging cobweb, the thick leaded pane, the carved mantle with 15 coats of white paint. They are telling me something, and always, it's as if the time I put into them will come back to me somehow.

After I returned to Bonaire, Hans—now the project manager of the renovation—with whom I'd been in intense communication with for all of May, and the first part of June, (77 emails in all), announced that he'd be going on vacation for two weeks. He assured me that he would leave clear instructions for Carrillo, the head builder. When Bonaireans go on vacation, they really go on vacation. Hans would not be available. This happened right at the moment when I would no longer have the extra time to agonize over tile lines and cabinet front patterns, paint colors, and whether or not the glass shutters on the kitchen door would whack into the exterior wall and break because nobody had thought about it. Why would I not? There is always a lot of competition for summer renters in my area of New York, so one really has to be on top of one's game. Hans leaving turned out to be another piece of luck. In June, the season in Sag Harbor was just getting into gear with showings. Then there was a quick success with our top floor apartment rental (July), which required us to move out, (guitars, basses, amplifiers, books, DVDs, video games, clothes . . .), into our first floor apartment, all the while having guests for the week, and showings for our August rental. If I had had to think about Bonaire during that time, I would have lost my mind, which is why I say I have a certain sort of luck with houses. My time and energy were not required at exactly the moment they were not available.

But back in February on Bonaire, when agent Anja and I were driving from one condo box to another, she had tried to steer me away from the idea of Kaya India, because it wasn't on the market, she said. The offer I later made from New York, based on the listings I had seen, was received with perplexity. For any agent, an offer on a house that isn't listed for sale is almost always going to be more work. In this case, on the phone that day, she sounded as though she'd never heard of such a thing. The owner would have to be located, she said, and they might not want to sell. And, where would they go? All of this would take a lot of time, she said. I lived far away, and this was a second home, all detracting from my potential "realness," the one quality desired above all others by real estate agents. For her, it would just be so much easier to get into a negotiation on a listed property.

The agents on Bonaire wouldn't really discuss it, but after 2008, the money had dried up there, like everywhere. In addition, the changeover in January 2012 from the NAF (Netherlands Antilles Florin) to the U.S. dollar had been hard on the economy. I heard from many people, and also saw that there are a lot of houses on the market, more on the high end than the low, some unfinished. And, construction companies and carpenters were out of work.

To solicit a seller that isn't a seller usually takes more money, even in hard times. Our first offer was turned down flat with no counter. I then went up, a lot, probably overpaying because I was so determined. With that second bump, they were interested, and things began to roll along briskly. Anja went on vacation, and the owner of the company took over the negotiations, with e-mails and document scans flying back and forth between us, technical inspector Hans, and the notary. The owner of Sunbelt Realty had no qualms or questions, getting back to me at the end of business every day. With the cheerful detachment typical to top-producing brokers, she just kept her mind on finalizing a deal. By the time Anja returned and took over again, we were just on the verge of signing a contract. Though she would be due a commission, she was still lukewarm and unenthusiastic during our conversations on the phone. Steve and I were really puzzled now. Was there something we didn't know about the house? The night before we signed, I was up until 3 a.m., wondering about it.

The original estimate from Hans, of about 30k, was to repair and replace the existing house at Kaya India. What was included, word for word: *Plastering and finishing the separation walls of the plot, plastering and painting the unplastered walls in the front, Retile the floors of the whole house to create a unity in material applications, applying the new tiles over the existing ones (62 m2, tiles supplied by owner), Paint the roof sheets and beams, (80 m2), and apply a moulding board 2X4, Repair the bad plaster around several windows, Build a double rinse tank on the side of the house, 2 basins of 60X60X4 cm, watertight, with drainpipes 2", Build a concrete floor as porch along the whole right side of the house (8,60 m long, and 3 m wide, about 3 cm. below the level of the living room, Give the whole house a paint job (225 m2), Finish the gypsum sheet ceilings and replace the soft board ceiling of the rear bedroom (9 m2) including moulding strips (5 lengths available), Remove the existing shower set in the bathroom, Apply a new (supplied by owner) shower set, Make an (outside) provision for a washing machine and a gas bottle and waste container, demolish and remove the kitchen block, plugging water lines, demolish and cart away front platform, extend the capacity of the electrical installation, with more outlets, and 220/240V wiring and outlets (count on 6 220V outlets, and an extra 4 127 outlets, Remove all old exterior door and windows.* All calculated at about $21,700. Then I would have the price of the burglary-proof windows and doors, ($9,600, installed) and the price to replace what they called the "kitchen block" ($2,000). The contract was modified to remove the work on the separation walls of the plot, because we decided we wanted to oversee that when we were there, and we didn't think we'd need a walled garden in order to live there. So Hans was on the mark—about $31,300 for what he had sent to me in his preliminary estimate. That is, about $30,000 to restore a simple, very modest village house, make it burglary proof, do nothing to the bathroom except replace the shower and add a shower heater, restore the kitchen as it was, and add on a porch to increase the living area without having to get permits. No trellis on the porch, no air-conditioning, no ceiling fans (wiring and fixtures), no upgraded septic, no Wi-Fi or cable, (the house had never had a phone), no heater for the shower (many on Bonaire do without it), no decent-sized kitchen, and of course no furniture, no appliances, no landscaping. On the day I met Hans, he emphasized more than once how small the house was, that it was a "simple job." Still, I spent a lot of time while I was on Bonaire, picking out the kitchen cabinets, the doors and windows, and looking at the very limited selection of appliances. Once I was back in New York, there was a tremendous amount of research to do, phone calls to make, decisions to be made. It's one thing to do a simple job that one can oversee every day, and another to do it from 2,000 miles away. Even if you have a general contractor, most people try to get on the site at least a few times a week. In Sag Harbor, many people hire a general contractor and check in every day, hovering, sometimes to the annoyance of the general contractor. Not to do so is to invite years of regret. For example, a friend of mine had specially ordered a Victorian claw foot tub to install perpendicularly against an angled wall of her old house, in front of the one large window in the bathroom. Her vision was to overlook the tops of the trees of her garden from the tub. Sadly, the crucial question of which end the tub trim should go on wasn't asked, and the job was expensively plumbed with the trim on the window side of the tub. So now, when my friend takes a bath, she looks out over the toilet and washbasin instead of the tops of trees as she had envisioned. It would be fine if she were the type that didn't care. She isn't. A mistake like this can shorten a lifetime.

Agent Anja, so tentative in April, had the most perfect English of anyone I spoke to on Bonaire. Perhaps her facility with language illuminated for her the obstacles I might encounter. As we went on with the job, I thought of her often. It isn't so much language problems one encounters, as language discrepancies. They can be very small. The only way to cope with it is to listen, carefully, to the rhythms and the usage one encounters, to use the words *they* use as much as possible, while hoping at least that you have a similar meaning in mind, and watch for the instances where they don't.

That everything is mostly on e-mail *can* be helpful. It gives one the time to study it and figure it out. Another tactic is to write everything out on an e-mail as clearly as if you were addressing a five-year-old.

Leading to e-mails such as this:

Hello Hans: Wanted to let you know that there are horizontal texture "lines" on the brown fronted kitchen cabinets I picked. I'm attaching a picture of the grey tile I chose, and how I would like it positioned—the "lines" on the tile should be horizontal, like the cabinet texture "lines." So, if I were coming in the existing front sliding door, and walking straight back to the kitchen, I would have the tile under my feet, the pattern on the tile going from the bedroom side to the porch side. This is really important to my design . . . And this:

Hi Hans: Thank you. I paid the invoice for the doors and the fans on May 31st. Yes, the exterior color is too dark but glad to hear it can be fixed. Please remember that the sink should go right under the kitchen window on the back wall. I did find a refrigerator small enough when I was there, at City Shop. It needs a 220 volt outlet. Yes I'd like the fan over the living room area, in the middle, 25% of the distance from the front wall to the back wall. See the attached diagram. It looks like the porch is higher than we discussed, it looks great. Is it level with the interior floor? Please let me know.

Everything is in millimeters and meters, not feet and inches:

Hi Hans: Great about the tiles. If you can take more wide-angle pictures of the whole house when you have a moment, I'd appreciate it. Also, if the sliding door has to be half meter less wide, I'd like a half meter MORE of wall space towards the kitchen, rather than towards the front of the house. That is, keeping the same position of the door that we discussed, with the same amount of wall space, (1.5 meters) between the front edge of the door and the front wall. Let me know if this is possible. Lastly, can you send a picture of how the interior, tiled floor is meeting the porch floor?

Somehow, the lack of one's physical body *on* the island increased the chances that one's order, from the only decent window and door company on the island, Alubon, would be put into the "maybe later" file.

Hi Hans: I called and spoke to the salesperson at Alubon earlier this week. It sounds as though they are very backed up there. They still have not emailed me, or called me. I'm beginning to worry that the windows and doors won't be done and installed on time, and as you know, I have to be absolutely finished by August 1. Is there another option for windows and doors on the island? There must be.

A little bit of helplessness is good:

Hi Hans: Thanks for all. I remember that Alubon was manufactured on the island, and so, it must be a shorter time for them than the other people, and also, I'm not ordering anything fancy . . . I can't imagine why they don't seem to want to take my order. I will have to have a direction to go in re: windows and doors by Tuesday at the latest. I'll call the other people at Regimac on Monday, maybe there's something you can do about Alubon. I'm ready to make a down payment on an order now.

It also helps to do a lot of underlining and "bolding," saving these effects for when they are really needed:

Hi Hans: Re: the (1) contract referring to (2) Offers - The offers will have to be negotiated and re-done as soon as possible before I will sign the contract.

*There should be a credit for the doors, b/c **I'm providing them**. I should just be paying labor.

*($400) for 6 roof sheets. Can it really be that much? Replacing them all was estimated at $2,000 in the recommendations part of the technical inspection.

*I want to confirm that if we want a **specific color paint** for the exterior of the house, that will be included.

*The **contract** should include that I reserve the right to withhold the last **30%** percent of the total fee until I'm satisfied that the windows and doors are in and the work is completed and the <u>ground and the interior of the house are free of construction debris</u>. In addition, the language in the contract about the work on the windows and doors isn't clear. <u>What should be included is everything that will be done to prepare the house for the installation of the windows and doors, as per the plan and measurements I described in my email to Alubon.</u> On the north side of the house, there will be a sliding door installed, toward the front of the house. The existing north window will be taken out and the wall repaired/filled in. The two kitchen windows will be made larger, the bathroom window larger, as per the measurements. The front slider will be taken out and the wall prepared for a new window to match the other front window. If you look at the Alubon quote you will see that **Alubon won't pay for: "construction work such as ground, chop, break, dismantle, cement, paint, repair or any other construction or carpenter work," so I need to know that everything will be done to prepare the house for the installation of the windows and doors for $650.**

I knew from previous jobs that the very first thing one does is get the windows and doors ordered, because they take the longest to make. When I was trying to negotiate the contract and get the window order in from New York, there had been a massive blackout on Bonaire, but I'm sure my order had languished for some time before that. Burglary-proof windows and doors have been brought to a new, stylish level in the Caribbean, especially when fabricated by the elusive Alubon company. Hans had taken me there to meet with the salesperson, who described everything in detail, and showed me the little factory where they make the louvered windows and doors with glass shutters that are their specialty. Each of the glass shutters has a steel bar inside it, welded to the aluminum frame. The most diligent thief, she said, could not get through the bar barehanded or with any kind of tool. The windows, in fact, have the same protection as the steel bars one sees in high crime areas in the U.S., but the glass shutters don't give it away. They can be open or shut to any degree, to control the amount of light and flow of air, and come in bronze, green, opaque white, and something called "Satinato," for a diffused, creamy light inside the house. We decided on green, which she described as "like sunglasses for the house," and would be cooling. She suggested a light yellow for the exterior color of the house that would go well with the green glass and the white aluminum frames of the windows and doors, for a tropical look. The idea is one has a house like Fort Knox, that doesn't look like a jail.

But back in April, everything was on track to a totally unknown destination. I was haunted by agent Anja's half-heartedness. I hate to look weak or undecided, especially after having gotten myself so thoroughly wedged inside a self-created nightmare. So I resisted calling her back. Eventually, having trouble putting pen to paper on the contracts, I dialed her number, and in an un-business like flurry of emotion, asked why she was so cool about Kaya India. *Didn't she think it was a good deal?* Yes she did, she replied, somewhat wearily. *It's a good location, right?* Yes, she replied, with more verve. *Then what's the problem?* "Oh Rue," she blurted out, "we spent a lot of time together, and so I feel like I know you. I just think you would be much happier with a place that doesn't need so much work!!"

In New York, all the details pertaining to the house just kept coming. First, I had to set up an account in MCB Bank Bonaire and get—miracle of all miracles—internet access to it. It took two visits when I was there,

12 e-mails, four phone calls, and two Skype calls before I could actually log on. Then there was setting up the assessment the cable/TV/internet company, Telbo, (two visits in person, eight e-mails, four phone calls, still not done), for installation and then, once installed, trying to tease apart the archaic boondoggle of their billing system. Then there was setting up a way to pay WEB, Water and Energy Bonaire, where I must call every month on the 29th, the day the house transferred, to get the bill and transfer the amount from MCB. This was imperative because the mail from Bonaire takes eight to ten weeks, and if I dropped that particular ball, the workmen would have no electricity for their power tools. It was sweet of Anja to worry about how it would go for us. It was a lot of work. I wouldn't recommend it to anyone who doesn't have real time to put into it, some experience, and a complete office setup where they don't mind spending many weeks.

As July rolled around, the renovation was almost complete. We bought plane tickets, and were due to arrive on Bonaire in a little over a month. We planned to stay for three and a half weeks, furnishing the house, finishing the kitchen, deciding how we'd do the garden, the garden walls, and finding a house manager for the rental. Emmett and I would snorkel and see the reef together and take wind surfing classes on Lac Bay, which we heard is a great place to learn the sport. Steve would be interested in the restaurant row, on Kaya Jan N.E., a ten-minute walk away from the house. He would want to know about the live music in the clubs. I knew he'd love Gio's Gelato for the coffee, and setting up the kitchen and barbeque, and identifying birds. We ordered *Birds of the Netherlands Antilles* by K.H. Voous. Still available, though out of print, it is the most detailed bird guide for the area. I hoped to see a few giant iguanas because Emmett would love that. We'd have time to get to know Bonaire better; delicious wads of time rolled out in front of me in our future paradise. I couldn't wait.

But as I walked our dog Rosie, and shuttled Emmett back and forth from baseball practice, I wondered, were we in a field of clover? Or was it just that I *felt* that we were lucky? On our meanderings around town, I did trust that some of the time, but not all the time. As I said, I am impulsive and visionary by nature; I don't care if things don't fit. In fact, things are more interesting to me when they don't. At that point, the more grown up side of me chimes in, arguing, *Hey, we only get one life, and one set of resources. It's limited. Don't be an idiot.* Which led me to ponder good fortune in all of its variety. There is the kind that is self-created, where good things materialize as a well-tended plant grows, or a beloved child thrives. Then there's the sort of luck that seems to drop from the sky, not wished for or even conceived of, winding through the days unsurprisingly, knitting them together into a coherent form that later looks like some sort of a plan or a reward for virtue. But it isn't. One type of luck you make, and the other you hope for, and like Christmas lights the different kinds get tangled up. One light goes out, and the whole string goes black. Or a bulb is replaced, and a part of the string that was dead lights up again. Being able to live in a beautiful mansion in the Catskills in college is an example of the second kind of luck. Would it stay with me? I thought of it often in those waiting Sag Harbor days.

Bonaire, August

On red-eye flights, I much prefer a long one. A short one is sort of a joke sleep. No matter how many pillows and drinks, one doesn't have the time to fully give in to the contortion of trying to sleep upright. It's sort of a fitful pre-sleep all the way through, perhaps because of knowing that after what passes for dinner (cold, miserable sandwich), it will be only a few hours till touchdown.

Feeling groggy, Steve, Emmett, and I deplaned down a long set of stairs onto the tarmac, the breeze soft, the sky an inky black punched with stars. After getting through customs, we drove along the main seaside road, J.N.E. Craane, lined with great black hulking shapes of the sort of condos I had rejected. On the other side, the sea was shrouded in a muted violet, as if reluctant about the approaching day. As much as I could be in the dark, I was finely tuned to every nuance of their faces, especially Steve, who had put pen to contract on a house that he'd never been inside of, in a country in which he had never set foot. We were due to meet Hans and get the tour and a set of keys at 8:00 a.m. In the meantime, we drove all around the island. I took them up to the Caribbean Club where I had seen hummingbirds, I took them by a complex that had a one-bedroom condo that I'd decided not to buy, I took them by our house and around the neighborhood more than once—5:00 a.m., 6:00 a.m., 7:00 a.m. The house was half-painted that strange ochre yellow that head builder Carrillo had chosen, hearing at some point "yellow" and not waiting for the shade. We were later to discover that that was a pattern with him.

I was relieved to see that the shutters and windows were in, however with no screens, because Alubon had waited until the very last minute. The house, surrounded with packed dirt that had not been turned over in years, looked as if it had sprung up in a moon crater. I searched for a reaction from either one, but I couldn't really tell what they thought. With Steve, that's typical. Sometimes I'm not sure he even knows what he thinks. It is also true that many people conjure up opinions that aren't really theirs. They reach, sometimes prematurely, for an image, an association, or a reference point. Children are for the most part free of this tendency. Steve is free of it. He surmises very rarely, which, though frustrating, is never false. As we crept around the locked house, peeking in windows, me squealing with delight at how different it all looked, he merely nodded. Emmett looked sort of stunned.

I was happy at how big the porch was; 30 square meters was more than I'd thought. I was however aghast at the property's size—.17 of an acre isn't that much, but with no design and hardly any vegetation, a square of dirt with a house plunked down in the middle of it looks bald and undefended. As we wandered around, the eastern trade winds picked up with the growing heat and sun. A pair of parakeets flew under the trellis, a streak of green and orange. I noticed the apartment building next door, windows looming, and thought about ways to block their view. I quickly consulted my native trees book about the trees we did have. One wayaka, very old. Two tamarinds. A small sea grape in the corner. In the back, also in the corners, two neem trees, which are considered large weeds on Bonaire, I was later to find.

The first day was what we called kamikaze house finishing at its best. Though Anja and Hans said we should find a hotel for a few days, we didn't, not wanting to spend the money. And because I knew that roughing it would force us to faster action. There was no furniture, no kitchen sink, no fridge, no stovetop, no washer, running water only in the bathroom sink and the rinse tanks outside on the porch. No drawers, no closets. No screens on the windows, no curtains, no screen on the sliding door. No heater for the shower, and a shower drain that didn't work, so no shower. The only real plumbing was the rinse tanks out on the porch—two big concrete boxes plugged with sections of PVC pipe and a crude drain that exited from side of the house into the dirt.

There's always a moment when turning on a spigot after a renovation. It's miraculous, the way the water flows into the pipe and from the mouth of the faucet, summoned by a twist of the hand. In my state of exhaustion, I let it flow over my hands and splashed it over my head, feeling "the bones" of the house— that the pipes ran from the main on the street, under the turned up ground, through and over its concrete walls, that the meter in the street box whirred away, registering how much was used, and that the water was fresh and good. The same, but different. No chlorine, absolutely pure. On Bonaire, the tap water is almost always lukewarm. Hans had brought us an ice chest to borrow, which was thoughtful. He also took the time to introduce us to neighbors Caren, an American marine biologist who worked at the nearby CIEE, and her Dutch husband Frans. After dumping our suitcases in the bedrooms, we went out to buy beds, linens, towels, kitchen stuff, food, and last but not least, ice for the ice chest. We had to drive around to the few places there are and make quick decisions, in order to get the beds delivered that day, and then we had to go to three different places just to find ice, being referred on by each place to the next place. Fortunately, I had some idea of where all these places were. Anja, knowing what our situation would be, had e-mailed me a detailed list of where to get this and where to get that. This was invaluable because we had Saturday only, some of the places had limited hours, and on Sunday, everything would be closed. This was a small baptism into the true conundrum that is Caribbean Island living, in which we would be immersed in about a week.

Also on that first day we met Yvonne again, the woman who lives across the street, whom I had met in April. As before, she was very nice and welcoming, putting Emmett and Steve immediately at ease, the sort of person who knows everything that goes on and watches over all, but not in a meddlesome way. With a round face as sweet as a child's, she reminded me of someone I knew long ago in school, some little friend who hadn't an ounce of malice. A sheltering person. I could see that she wasn't that much older than me, but she had grandkids over, one boy near Emmett's age. Emmett was shy and so were we, as well as tired. I didn't feel up to the importance of the occasion of seeing her again. I wanted to be, as she was the only person in the neighborhood that I knew.

Once we had the beds and the ice, we went to the big new Dutch supermarket, Van den Tweel, and stopped at the cheap Chinese goods market for a rice cooker and coffeemaker. These turned out to be lifesavers. Of course, the coffee maker needed only electricity. Fortunately, we had some. We even had outlets above the countertop. Steve knew exactly what to do, because in his bad old days he'd cooked all his meals in a rice cooker in a rented room in Arizona. He rinsed the vegetables in the bathroom sink, cut them up on cardboard, and plunked the rice in. He let the rice cook to a certain point of chewiness, added the broccoli and carrots, and let the cycle finish out. We had some excellent Dutch chocolate too. We ate on paper plates, sitting on plastic deck chairs. Telbo had hooked us up the previous week and so, after figuring out the codes, we had Wi-Fi. We watched the Summer Olympics on the BBC, the computer propped up on the coffeemaker box.

After a relatively quiet Sunday walking around and swimming in the sea, we turned in early.

At 3:00 a.m., I was woken up by a donkey braying, that sounded as if it were just outside the window, a few feet away from my head. If I had brushed up against a large furry beast in bed next to me, the shock would've paled next to the initial jolt. A donkey braying sounds like a hacksaw stuck in a tree, wielded by a disturbed, violent, but ultimately ineffective person. One can hardly imagine that it is a love call, so strangled and pathetic are the tones, so *impotent* does it sound. So hopeless. Lying in bed, bones rattling, I wondered what donkeys could possibly be communicating to each other with it. I could only come up with existential dread. That they are a half-domesticated animal now makes them a conduit to existential dread for us.

Steve, lucky for him, was up getting a snack in the kitchen at the time of the donkey explosion. For him it wasn't that loud, he said. He was pretty certain it wasn't in the yard. He told me that in general, donkeys are loud, and that it could have been somewhere in the neighborhood and I would have heard it. We've seen donkeys in fields, and along the roadways, but certainly not in the yard. It is true that I'm sensitive to noise, always have been.

The third and fourth and fifth nights belonged to one dog, who I later named Bollocks for the size of his testicles, and his gall.

On Bonaire, most of the native Bonaireans and many of the long-term Dutch have dogs. These dogs are living burglar alarms, there in the yards to scare off the kids who prey on tourists. These thieving children will break into any home they think they have a shot at, to grab cameras, computers, phones, and TVs. There is no punishment or court for juveniles on the island.

For the first couple of nights, we heard the neighborhood dogs bark in packs a few houses to the east/northeast, a generalized, mass dog chorus of highs and lows, which would then go silent again, the urgent conversation amongst themselves eventually reaching a mysterious conclusion. On my first visit to Bonaire, when I had stayed a few streets over in the same neighborhood, and noticed the ebb and flow of sound. I found it bearable, even quaint. The dogs within audio reach of Kaya India #8 were about the same as then, the volume perhaps a few notches higher, as we were that much deeper in a more truly local area.

All this before Bollocks made his debut. I really shouldn't call him Bollocks because almost all of the dogs on Bonaire are not fixed, so there was no reason for him to stand out. Except that someone tied him up next to a carport on the other side of our wall. And he, very vocally, made his displeasure known. By barking alone, for hours, not tucked within a community of like-minded, reasonable fellows just keeping watch over things, but incessantly, loudly, independently in deep protest at his situation, interspersed with the howls, whimpers, and pleas of a forsaken soul.

He started on our third day, in the afternoon, and went on for several hours. Steve actually commented on it. "What's going on with that dog?" he asked. When Steve comments, something *is* strange. Sometimes I use whether he comments or not as a gage of how out of the ordinary a thing is. By the time Emmett and I returned from our afternoon swim, he said, "That dog is barking a lot," and Emmett said, "Yeah, he is." Steve didn't think we should, but Emmett and I snuck to the front corner of our yard to look through the fence into the neighbor's, where the sound was coming from. We found a rust-colored creature with eyes the color of toffee and balls to his knees, (if he had knees). For such a loud mouth, he cringed at just the sight of us and crawled under the car next to him as far as his rope would allow.

Obviously, the dog had been beaten for barking. Emmett thought that was sad and it was.

But, it didn't stop him from starting up again at about 9:30 that evening and continuing till midnight, taking an hour's break, and recommencing. Emmett, being a child, was sleeping with his head stuck under a pillow, (I know, I saw him at 2:00 a.m.). I crept back to bed, hoping that Steve was sleeping, listening for the telltale snore. If Steve was sleeping, that would mean that I was being oversensitive, and at some point, I would get used to this din. Didn't I want the authentic Bonaire experience? Didn't I find the roosters at daybreak and beyond sort of charming? Hadn't I brought a white noise machine just for the possibility of this sort of thing? I reached over and turned it up. But it was no match for Bollocks, whom I began to really hate. I wondered if people on Bonaire were drunk most of the time, or deaf from the dogs, or both. I wondered if I was having some sort of yuppie/culture clash problem, and that the ability to sleep alongside a howling, miserable beast was inherent in humans back to the cavemen, and that my semiprecious life in Sag Harbor had robbed me of this basic ability. As the pleading and barking went on, I lay awake mentally talking to this dog—what are you *thinking*, what do you *want*, if you could tell me *I'd do it*.

The next morning, very tired, I tiptoed around Steve, trying to determine if he had had the same sort of night. Into the day, the barking continued, only more, and we all began to talk about it, reveling in brief oases of silence where we could forget about this dog's problems. I thought the dog would exhaust himself and give up eventually, but that did not happen. Eventually all three of us went over to peek into the neighbor's deserted lair— open gate, driveway, car, a sad, caged monkey, big palm trees, and Bollocks tied up to the carport. So miserable. Upon seeing us, he whimpered, went under the car, and shut up. And then restarted, like an engine that couldn't stop turning over. It went on and off all afternoon, mostly on. As I lay in bed that night, I tried to think of how the dog was so timid and scared, in order to like him more, and incorporate his incessant complaints into the general cacophony of noise that is the world wherever one goes. I thought, this is just life as usual. I'm the sensitive one. If people on Bonaire can live with it, why can't we? No *other* house lights are on, on this fucking street. It's just us, the new Americans. They are watching us, thinking that that woman is crazy enough to be under a street lamp, at 3 a.m., trying to reason with a dog, while everyone is sleeping . . . Wagging a finger at the dog, giving the dog a Hitler salute, lunging forward in a Pilates plunge to try and scare some sense into it.

The next day Steve looked grumpy, and we were all sort of depressed, like people might be under siege. Bollocks went on, barely breaking to eat or drink. One solution was to close all the doors on that side of the house to create a sort of barrier to the noise, but at night that was no help. Because we had no air-conditioning yet, we couldn't shut the windows. The hours came and went. At 8:00 p.m., trying to watch TV on our computers in the bedroom, Steve looked at me and said, "We have to sell this house. Now. Put it on the market, TODAY."

"You're kidding."

"No, I'm not. I can't live with this."

"What about if I go across the street and talk to that woman, Yvonne? She must know those people."

"Don't. That isn't going to help. This is a cultural thing. If you stir things up, it will just draw attention to us that we don't want, and we'll rile things up with the neighbors. We don't want that."

Normally I have a quick comeback, but this was too serious. I left the room, aghast.

He really meant it. My heart was sinking. That afternoon I had seen, with Emmett, queen parrot fish, squirrel fish, blue tangs, juvenile blue tangs, a sharp tail eel, (silver with white spots), French grunts, a funny kind of flounder, (maculated) flat as a pancake, with two eyes on one side of its body and the ability disappear under the sand of the sea bottom in seconds. We saw all of this holding hands, (probably the last few times he would do that naturally), while slowly gliding around the pier, at a depth of no more than eight feet, stopping to watch the big tarpon glide by, Emmett ripping the mask off his face to express his delight. For him, it's not the detail of the fish that matters, it's the size.

Arguments with spouses can sometimes bring out the reasoning that was already there buried. All that's needed is the friction. I marched back into the bedroom.

"Steve, people are people. I find it extremely hard to believe that these people just go about their business without noticing this. On the other side of that house is a construction site, and across from it a house that's deserted. That's why it goes on. We're the closest to it, then Yvonne. She MUST be noticing this."

"You have no idea how people react or what they're used to. This isn't your country! The only solution is to put the house on the market."

"I will not! Just like that, without making a peep! Like, slink away with our tails between our legs? Oh yeah, go through all of this work and planning, and then just give up! That's ridiculous! I want to talk to her!"

"It's pointless. You don't want to get into it! How come she hasn't done anything? It isn't a good idea to move into a neighborhood you don't know in a country that isn't yours and start complaining. You'll just be ASKING for trouble."

I went back out to the living room. In our dirt yard, moon shadowed now, I could almost see an outline of my imagined garden—banana trees, a few types of palms, more wayakas, fruit trees, and the vines called "climbing yellow," along the porch railings and up over the trellis. Big planters of palms on either end of the porch, where our fins and masks were hung up to dry.

Just then, I saw that Yvonne had come out of her house and was on her porch, saying hello or goodbye to some members of her vast extended family. I was in my pajamas with no bra and no robe. The moment, however, shook me down. I went flying across the street, arms crossed to hide my relative nudity. She paused on her way back in.

"Yvonne, sorry. Can I talk to you?" She nodded with concern for what must have been the look on my face. I thought, women are so wonderful, the world over. We're all attuned to the same sorts of things. That men mostly don't notice. "We are having such a time of it . . ."

"Oh no, what?" she exclaimed.

"That dog . . . It's been days and nights . . . going on . . ." Her face came to life. "Yeeessss, I KNOW!!"

"Oh, thank God," I said. "I was wondering if it was just us!"

"Nooooo," she said. "I've thought the same thing. On and on, eet's going on and on!"

I was so relieved. If she could have known how relieved, she would've been surprised.

"She ties the dog up and they go to the other side of the house. I'll call her. Don't worry. I geev you my number if you need to call me." She got a pen and paper and wrote it down.

"Oh great! Thank you, thank you, Yvonne. We weren't sure . . ."

"Noooo, don't worry. I thought, you know, if could . . ." she made a pistol out of her hand, "I would just, POP!"

I laughed, obviously having had the same thought.

An hour or so later, the barking stopped. Steve and I took deep, cleansing breaths and looked at each other, daring to hope that the silence would hold, and went to bed.

A while later, Steve was getting juice in the kitchen and said in a loud whisper, "Come here, quick! Quick!" He never says that, I thought, hastening out of bed.

"Get Emmett!" he said, and I did.

Steve was standing in the living room, outlined in the porch light, his back to us. As I got nearer, I saw outside two, no, four sets of long fawn-colored ears pointing straight up, and then a gray muzzle or two emerged, and an assemblage of black, inquisitive eyes. Just off of the porch, there was a herd of five wild donkeys, one apparently pregnant. They stood there in stoic, donkey fashion, waiting, as if they expected one thing or the other to happen. We stood as still as they were. Emmett was thrilled. When nothing particularly did happen, the donkeys turned to each other in amazement. The two in front began jockeying to be closest to us, nipping each other with crazed expressions, "Hey man, get back. I saw these suckers first. These are *tourists* man." Steve, ever wary, backed a few paces away. But the donkeys became still again, five pairs of ears like question marks. I had read somewhere that donkeys on Bonaire suffer terribly in a drought, which we were in, and that people often give them water, so I told Emmett to go get a pot of water. Steve said, "Oh no we shouldn't." I said, "For the love of God why not?"

Emmett put the water on the edge of the porch and the first one drank silently, lifting his wet, grey muzzle from an empty pot almost as soon as he had begun. We did it again and again, running back and forth from the rinse tanks with all manner of vessels. Emmett was so happy with this cool adventure, where he got to take care of the donkeys. Emmett has never in his life been the kid that tortures the frog. Steve is the same. I've seen him get in the car with a "Have A Heart" mousetrap and drive to the middle of our area's woods to give a mouse the best chance at survival. I love animals too, but that night I was misty eyed with simple relief at the silence.

On Bonaire all the occupied houses are fenced and walled to keep in the dogs, and keep other dogs out, and possibly the iguanas, who will eat the plants, and the donkeys. Maybe there were some other invaders we hadn't learned about yet, but so far this was all I knew. We had holes in our front wall and no back wall to speak of, so in this area we were plainly lacking. Bonaire, despite its gentleness, does have a sense of the encroaching wild. There is a battle between man and nature, even domesticated nature, that has not yet been called. There are many who would say that man *is* natural, no less natural than the donkeys or iguanas. And that might still be true. But the things that man must have for his/her comfort and convenience tend to make places feel like the same giant living room, screening movies of wildlife 24 hours a day and piping in bird call sound tracks.

For now on Bonaire, the natural world has the most turf. Which I love. But ramparts must be in place. While the construction at Kaya India had gone on and possibly even before, and holes in the fence had been boarded up with ineffectual 2X4s, and gates had been left open for days. We have seen dogs, including Bollocks, hop over the front wall and trot through as if they owned the place. That was how the donkeys got in, and went a ways towards explaining their brazenness. Emmett thought the donkeys should come in and sleep in the living room. Steve put an immediate end to that idea. The donkeys, ears flicking, waited patiently for the next development. Clearly, they saw hopping up onto the porch and cadging some cereal as an option. The pregnant one lifted her velvety muzzle, droplets of water plashing onto the dusty concrete of the porch. Emmett touched her forelock; just under it, her eyes were a deep brown.

Once Bollocks had shut up, we were able to sleep through the nights. I even began to sleep more in tandem with sunrise and sunset, which is unusual for me. At the start of every day a milky light came in to wake me, followed by straight gold ribbons of sun tracing the walls, and angling around the corner into the living room.

Steve, ever a connoisseur of mornings, let me into this quiet world a little defensively. I tend to get my brain jumpstarted by talking, while he begins his day with a silent vigil in front of the computer for news and politics. He was particularly partial to a website that featured all the news from home. He would then give me dispatches about the record numbers of car accidents there were, or who had died that week. I told him, and he also knew, that I had gone to all this trouble in part to get away from local news and gossip. We have left our area of Long Island every summer for one month since Emmett was three years old. It's not that I hate where we live, it's just that the only way that I can contend with reality—the actual living, the being born, the months and years flying by, and the suffering in between—is to go away for one month out of the year and have a fantasy that the news and the inevitable are put on hold, or just plain erased. There's a warped logic at work—if I haven't participated, how can these things have happened? If I haven't heard it, how can it be true? The potential of this approach is unlimited. It is amazing what one can temporarily choose to forget, while knowing that the pretense of adulthood will eventually need to be conjured again. That knowledge can get pretty small, a mere speck. If one forgets adequately enough, there is an illusion within the illusion—a delicious one of having no timeframe at all. The far off duty melts and morphs into the space all around it, disappearing entirely from view.

It wasn't though, as if we didn't have to accomplish anything. It's just that it was all finite and contained. No opening up mail and going down the rabbit hole of say, a tax audit. Just a few things every day. A list compiled at dawn, then checking through as many things on the list as possible by dusk, while adding in something else, like swimming, walking, or walking into the town to eat, or driving over to the other side of the island to the beach. Setting up the furniture, the kitchen, the garden. It was just like playing house as a kid. Among new things happiness is foretold, and seems to repeat itself indefinitely.

My favorite thing to do was to watch the bird action over the house at 6:30 a.m., which is rush hour in the bird world. The yellow-shouldered Amazon parrots called loras, flying in pairs and groups, parakeets in pairs, tropical mockingbirds, and troupials, shooting across like arrows, following some inner compass, proceeding only as nature dictates. The dark, silver blue of the sky is alive with activity in the morning, while slowly succumbing to a wash of pearl from the east.

Alex Dzierba

There was much to carry here and there, so last week we traded in our rental car for a flatbed truck. In a few weeks we had accomplished a wicker sofa and chairs, and a custom-made TV stand and four bedside tables by a Dutch artist, fashioned from salt-bleached ship timber from the Netherlands. Because of space limitations, the tables in the bedrooms had to be identical, and it's almost impossible to find four of any one thing. The stand had to fit exactly into the corner of the living room, and hold books as well. To make a small space work, every millimeter has to be utilized.

Hans Rietveld, taken up with the sewer project in the town, was no longer on the scene. Head carpenter Carrillo, the finish carpenters, and the sub-contractors had to deal with me directly, and, just like in the States, there are problems. They don't want to take direction from a woman. Also, they know I probably won't give them work again, so they can be flakey and/or exploitive. Most are Venezuelan, here just to work, and so there are language problems. They don't have the smattering of English that many Bonaireans have. Steve speaks some Spanish, thank God, and had to be the intermediary, a position he hates. He was also guilty about being the boss and was sometimes overfriendly, and then hurt when they tried to take advantage. I was less surprised.

Then there were the costs. Even though the house was not very complicated, essentially just shoebox of about 750 square feet, the finishing touches ran into the multi-thousands. Light fixtures, table lamps, a washer, the shower heater, outdoor furniture, a refrigerator, a transformer for the refrigerator to regulate the 220 volts it runs on. (The 220 current on Bonaire is inconsistent and can burn out a fridge motor quickly.) Everything is high—a laminate Ikea-style bureau with a beachy wood finish: $450. Cutlery, $35 for four place settings. Wicker bathroom caddy: $90. A collapsible rack to dry clothes on: $40. A small plain bathroom mirror, such as one would find in a train bathroom: $25. And TOWELS—at least $18 for the lowest grade, rough, Chinese-made strip of fabric that deposits pills and leaky rivulets of dye all over one's body without even accomplishing the job of absorbing water. Fabric, ceramics, plastics, wood, electronics . . . everything was phenomenally expensive.

Yet, the dearth of goods gave us opportunities to be environmentally prudent. For example, the house came with a shoddy, jerry-built closet in the front bedroom, which had a lot of unused space above it. The shelves were plywood that snagged material, the louvered doors of the cheapest pine. Instead of three door panels, there were two, and so on. An American carpenter would have said to me, first thing, "Let's rip it all out and start over," but the Venezuelan carpenter wanted to reuse almost everything. His list of additional materials was small and pricey, and his labor cheap by U.S. standards. He took the time to find the door that would match the others, and built out the top to the ceiling to make an "owner's closet" with a sliding door and pop lock. The plywood was sanded and varnished, the doors the same. In the U.S., labor is expensive and materials cheap. By ripping everything out, the American would have to spend more time at it, driving up his bill, and it well might be an easier job for him that way.

But an island is a contained market. There's no competition, there are few subsidies. The materials are expensive because the fuel and labor to get them there by boat are figured in. We, the environmentally minded, get a consummate thrill out of NOT buying stuff, cherishing what is re-purposed, what is useful for a lifetime or more. I was happy that the wood didn't end up in the dump. The whole exercise felt in line with the future, when our world will become more like an island, the price of goods and materials aligning with the actual costs of producing them. I also noticed that this market-driven environmentalism came at the expense of the worker doing the job, because he can only charge what the market will bear after material costs. Maybe we will all eventually become subject to the management of the physical world around us, to the ebb and flow of real things, materials, and resources that we hold in our hands, rather than company valuations that are anyway becoming more and more abstract. The heyday of our dominion is surely becoming archaic. It will have to, as the world gets ever smaller.

Alex Dzierba

Captain Don and Janet

The first two weeks of August had passed, and the appliances and furniture had been bought and installed. The next thing was to turn our attention to the dog and donkey stockyard that was our land up to this point. The house was beginning to look welcoming and wonderful inside, but the inhospitable crater that surrounded us needed lots of attention.

From almost the first day, Hans and Yvonne, and new friends Frans and Caren from down the street, had pointed out that our plot (they call them plots, not lots), was at a lower grade than the street and the surrounding properties. And we did notice that the ground looked as though it had lost much of its top layer. What was there was so hard-packed and stony that a shovel was useless, Steve had to take a chip axe to it. All of these people said that the yard would become a muddy pool in the rainy season, which might also threaten the stability of the house. As if custom ordered, a rainy day did come, and the local pig trotted through the hole in the wall and frolicked for a bit in the pool the rain had left. When it rains on Bonaire, it's like buckets pouring from the sky. Indeed, something would have to be done.

Enter the head builder Carrillo, who knew somebody, who knew somebody, an absolutely trustworthy fellow whom he had known for years. This fellow, with his dump truck, would pick up and deliver 100 square meters of soil and spread it out, which would bring the grade of the yard to the surrounding grade. The description went thus: *Fill the yard of the house and extend the soyle completely to level the floor of the yard,"* and *"The work consist of one hundred square meters of soyle a loader that will spread out the soyle in the yard and a man power for the places that the loader cannot reach."* We signed the contract and the loader came but, to everyone's surprise, 100 square meters only filled about 30 percent of the yard. So we had to get another 100 s2. And then another. As the first estimate, though incorrect, looked reasonable, we hadn't bothered to get a competing one. We were stuck with them, with no time to ponder on our way to the bank. We were either the victims of incompetence, being played like violins, or some combination of the two. It's true that I have in the past been accused of being too literal. This especially galled me as a real estate agent in the States. When I was starting in that business, my mentor as much as told me so. Apparently, the key to real estate is finding the vast grey areas that exist between words, whether they be spoken or written down. I was too literal because I look at a bunch of words on a page and even if the grammar is terrible, I take them to mean what they say they mean. I saw then that interpreting language in business is a sort of art, and on Bonaire, my respect for these illuminating powers was made new all over again. Our head builder, with almost no English at all, and a sort of Juan Valdez, moustache-twirling, cigar-chomping smile on his face, was a master, rendering my years of painstaking, hairsplitting study of the meanings of words useless. And he was charming too. We had become quite fond of him, before a series of events made us never want to see him again.

The stuff they deliver is called diabase. It raised the grade of the yard by about four inches while draining what was left in our bank account. After the last load, our yard did look much better and slightly more hopeful, with the aspect of a Zen sand garden that had just been gone over with the little spindled rake.

Steve knows a lot about gardening in the U.S., but the plants are very different here. Bonaire isn't considered tropical, but it isn't arid either. There is a short rainy season in the fall, which made it a good time to plant. We also had a bit of a start from neighbors Frans and Caren at the end of the street. Frans made us a lovely gift of four agave plants from their garden, and Steve planted them in a neat row on the street side of the front wall, lining up with the front view of the house.

During the finish work, I spent a lot of time walking and jogging around in the neighborhood, looking at gardens and taking pictures and thinking about the sort of thing that would appeal. Steve lived in the southwest for a long time, and likes cactuses and other plants that can endure in a harsh terrain. I'm not so crazy about cactuses, but realized it's merely a matter of getting a feel for them. There are tall cactuses that have a stark beauty on their own, and those, that planted together, can provide texture and varying greens and even flowers. And I loved the idea of a few palms. Palms are great for the sound they make in the wind, and because, unless they are sad and brown, there is something sexy about them. What? A sexy tree, you say? Yes, palms are sexy. Because they grow near the beach, they like it warm, they are regal and strong, but soft and whispery, especially at night, in the breeze. The movement they make in the sky is a loose-limbed ballet. A canopy of palms high above one's house, rustling in the wind, not far from open water of some kind, is about the closest thing to heaven that I can imagine.

But palms are not native to Bonaire. They don't provide any food for the birds. They have to start off small, unless one is willing to shell out hundreds and hundreds, which we no longer had. In fact, everything has to start off small, and be tended at first and watered regularly. Even the lovely, strong, native trees that we did have, surviving perfectly well without irrigation, got their start as un-trampled shoots, serendipitously poking out their tops at the start of a long ago rainy season. Lucky us, the rainy season was due to start in September. We had only about two weeks left on Bonaire, so there was much to be done.

We knew we'd have to start with saplings, *immediately*, because trees are the bones of a garden and they take a while to grow. But where, how, what?

Our new friends and neighbors, having steered us up to this point, saw that we were onto the next phase. Again, they all had the same advice: Captain Don's. *They'll help you out. Explain everything. What are the hours? Oh, just go there on a weekend. It's called Island Grower. There's a gate, ring the bell. Janet, his wife, is always there. Really, that's it? Yes, they know everything. Well how do we get there? On the road to Lagoen, you'll see a sign on the left.*

The small sign said only "Captain Don." Since the place wasn't officially a storefront or in a town, we felt strange about just driving in. Fenced all around, it looked like someone's very private property. At the end of the long drive was a big gate and a bell, which Emmett rang enthusiastically. Out came Janet, with a smile and a grey sweep of short hair, and two friendly mutts. She was in shorts and a little tank top, very fit and toned, not (I guessed) from an exercise regimen but from being outside all the time and running this place. Behind her there was an open-air potting and tool station, and big partial-shade greenhouses stretching in different directions. To our left, a lovely, old growth grotto with a bench inside, the sort of sheltering place with massive trees I'd like to have one day at Kaya India. Though, I reflected, that that might be a long way off. To the right, a makeshift compound of sheds bore the human touch, as they were fashioned largely from reused materials, and were very neat and organized.

We explained our situation, the big plot, the looming apartment building, the dwindling budget. With a fraction of my attention, I noticed that Emmett was more fidgety than usual, hopping from foot to foot, looking around hungrily. I told him to go play and explore, like children do. Janet was a fast study, understanding the depth of our ignorance by about sentence number five, while Steve began to get the pained look he does when he thinks I'm talking too much, which is always at an early point in any conversation. Then Emmett was hitting my arm, interrupting me, hopping around, "Mom, Mom!" along with making some little pained sounds that sounded to me as if he was bored.

"Emmett! I'm talking! Lots of iguanas here, I bet!" I said with an irritated sweep of my arm.

Janet said, "Yes, go ahead! Go play! There's lots to do!"

Eyes glued to me, Emmett didn't seem to want to leave, and was getting more agitated by the minute.

We resumed, keen to return to the issue of the garden. The worst time for children is when grown-ups are getting acquainted, engaged in the effort of storytelling and reading cues and signals by which we decide who the other one is. Children are incredulous at the intensity of this effort. Why am I suddenly invisible? Why are you so serious? Why the *affectation* of taking pleasure, when you are as grave as dogs sniffing each other out?

Emmett was starting to hop around like the ground was on fire, "Ow!! Owwww!!!! *OWWWW!!!!!!!*" he yelled.

"What's going on?" I yelled.

"Fire ants!" exclaimed Janet, grabbing a nearby bottle of vinegar solution.

Though he was barely able to stand still for the treatment, she dribbled it over his feet and along the sides of his calves, while the four of us moved toward the greenhouse paths. She talked about different sorts of natural remedies for fire ants in the ground and how pesticides don't really work on them. Still focused on Janet, I agreed that we don't like pesticides either, that it's always best to use natural substances if you can. Emmett thought he deserved more attention and sympathy than he was getting.

We ambled down paths through acres of plants, trees, and bushes roofed with the black plastic netting they call shade cloth. At the center of the operation, dwarfed by another huge tree, was a rustic, house and porch. This was where Janet and Captain Don worked and lived.

Originally from Hollywood, the son of an inventor and an actress, Captain Don's given name is Donal Stewart, though people on the island know him mainly as Captain and sometimes Sir, because was knighted by Queen Wilhelmina, brought into the order of Orange-Nassau of the Netherlands. This is because he almost single-handedly created the dive industry on Bonaire, which, along with St. Eustatius and Saba, is part of the Kingdom of the Netherlands. After spending a lot of time with him, I guessed that he wasn't taking his knighthood very seriously.

He arrived at what he cheerfully called "this rock" on his 17-foot schooner, the *Valerie Queen*, in 1962, with 63 cents in his pocket. Previously, he had been on Curacao with his mate Percy, scuba diving and collecting small aquarium fish. When Curacao immigration rejected them for a longer stay, they headed out for Antigua, stopping on the way on Bonaire, and finding it appealing for a "strong Dutch influence . . . and friendly people . . . " as he wrote in his book *Reef Windows*.

In 1962, there were only about 4,000 inhabitants on Bonaire, and no tourism industry nor any ideas for one. The Captain and Percy immediately made themselves busy with the aquarium fish and adventuring under the sea. As the concept of recreational diving was relatively new, they were among the first to see the splendor of Bonaire's underwater terrain. Plotting out an area, marking it with buoys or other devices, is what Don called making a "reef window." At that time, Bonaire's extensive reef system had not been mapped or even described. Don and Percy's reef windows enabled access and provided a description of the area's characteristics, though they didn't yet have a fixed idea of why they were doing it. They were just hooked on the fun of underwater exploration, marking places they could go back to. At this early stage, they had to import tanks of compressed air from Curacao, as there were no compressors on Bonaire.

Besides the heartbreaking beauty of forests of elkhorn, flower, mountainous star coral and a multitudinous variety of sea life, they discovered odd things like so-called "shoots," which had operated as garbage dumps for decades. "Everything, garbage . . . dead donkeys . . . a lotta sharks . . . a million broken bottles just waiting to slip over the edge of the subterranean cliff into the 3000 foot deep Wekua Trench," wrote Don. There were coral-encrusted urns hundreds of years old, piles of chamber pots from early ships, sunk fishing boats, and even a few shipwrecks. With 25 miles of unexplored leeward reef, and very few people to inhibit them from going anywhere they pleased, the Captain and Percy were busy and having a blast. Hurricane season was on the way, and the *Valerie Queen*, moored in the calm waters off of Kralendijk, was safe, because Bonaire is out of the hurricane belt. So they decided to delay the trip to Antigua a little more. The governor granted them an extension of their papers, though he added a condition, that they not cause trouble and find ways to improve the tiny island and the lot of its citizens. He actually pointed at the horizon and said,

"A nuisance you go . . . but if my island is a better place because of you, then . . ."

An idea of a business began to formulate, and soon they founded Bonaire Marine Tropical N.V. Though at first it was mainly spearfishing and trapping and exporting aquarium fish, they offered scuba too, and were sometimes taken up on that offer by intrepid vacationers. For a long time, they still had to import the compressed air from Curacao.

At the time there was only one hotel on the island, called Zee Bad (Sea Bath), built from the remains of a German internment camp from the forties. Don was hired to manage it, and quickly found that the mainstay of the job was drumming up diving business. This suited him very well. He hosted parties, sponsored boat races and regattas, and engaged clientele in naming his favorite unnamed windows. "La Dania's Leap," "1,000 Steps," and "Snake Valley" were all named by Don and his groups. After spending the day at the dive, they would return to the hotel and "immortalize that particular window . . ." With a plaque? No. With a ceremony? No. Don's method of immortalization was always a revel of some kind, which can be ceremonious depending on your way of looking at it.

Don thought that boats and guides were too expensive and largely unnecessary, as so much of Bonaire's reef could be accessed with just a truck and a map. He thought that people should be able to dive where and how they wanted, and wanted to remove as many obstacles as posible between them and the underwater world he so loved. That is how the concept of diving freedom was born. Don would truck vacation divers and their gear to a spot, many marked by little signs or painted stones as they are today, and they'd access the reef simply by walking out from the shore.

After walking a while, the greenhouse path gave way to another clearing where we met the Captain. He was in a wheelchair from a diving accident years before. He was bronzed all over, wearing only what appeared to be a small blue bathing suit. His left leg ended about 10 inches below the knee. At 85 years old, he was a weather-beaten Errol Flynn, still projecting some of the swashbuckling attitude of that movie star. In fact, he regularly assumes a pirate persona, adding a wooden peg leg and eye patch to complete the costume. He had an open face and a flinty gaze. A certain wickedness played about his smile and eyes, which I interpreted to mean that finding the humor in something was as important to him as any business at hand.

We told him our story, and I could see right away that he found it amusing, and maybe even interesting. As I recited the facts, I felt it that it was a bit of a test. Janet explained to him about the one visit and the purchase of the house, while Don had a quality of having been so long on what he and Janet call their *kunuku*, that he was as much a part of its fabric as the birds, plants, and iguanas. His big blue eyes traveled the length of each one of us, the strange interlopers, who had entered his and Janet's world by way of the search for adventure, same as he had done long ago.

Eventually, an aura of the old sage overtook him, and he nodded with a pursed little smile that made me think of some other movie star (Mickey Rourke? Tom Waits?). People who came fell in love with Bonaire in a week and went mad, buying houses and so forth? What sorts of people were they? Why, they were people like him, he seemed to be thinking. *We* were people like him, and that was pretty cool. As he wrote in *Reef Windows*, "Six months on Bonaire was like six months on nowhere. However, there was something about the place that held us . . . " Four decades later, I had a sense of being as far away as he did—"nowhere" but in a good way, like a writer or a spy might disappear into Africa or the Middle East for a few decades, turning up when everyone thought I was dead, the aura of real secrets clinging to my person, the pitfalls of absolutely connected, global living replaced with the mystery of having been mainly preoccupied with tangible things.

Janet said, "Don? They're in Kralendijk, near CIEE."

"How much land?" he asked for the second time.

"715 square meters," said Steve.

Eyebrows raised, "That's a big piece for that area," he said.

Janet invited us to sit down around the big dining table on the porch, and chatted away through the kitchen's open window. The interior of the house was as open to the outside as possible, with shade cloth rolled up along the many windows to encourage the breeze. No air-conditioners, nary a fan. Funny talismans to Don's diving years, along with plaques and awards were nailed up here and there on the exterior wall under the porch. The living rooms were filled with bookcases and an extensive DVD library.

Janet very kindly got water for everyone and snacks for Emmett. On Bonaire one is very thirsty, especially in summer when the days are long. Emmett, now free of fire ants, found some hermit crabs crawling around dumbly in the sunshine, in the gravel just off the porch. We studied them for a bit, their eyes black seeds on stalks, thin antennae questing for information until, startled, they withdrew, like nothing so much as a sharp intake of breath.

Don got out a pen and began to sketch out the plot, asking questions about the position of the house, the street, and the existing trees. Steve, ever handy with the numbers, was able to somehow work back from the square footage and give the approximate dimensions of the plot in relation to the house, which was what Don needed to make a map.

We also spoke of U.S. politics, and the news of the day on Bonaire, which was mainly about WEB (Water and Electric Bonaire), possibly raising rates by 50 percent. Recently built new wind power turbines were supposed to reduce the costs of energy as well as be carbon neutral, but then there was a wind die off due to La Nina, and the old power generator burned down. The scuttlebutt was that the construction of the excessively luxurious new turbines was mismanaged, quite possibly making a few corrupt people rich, while increasing pressure on Bonaire's largely poor population. Don thought there might be an uprising of some kind if rates did rise, because they're already among the highest in the Caribbean.

All of this was interspersed with Don's stories, many of which he has written down.

He gave us photocopies of particular ones that he thought were appropriate for our personalities, inscribing something on the covers, sometimes with a little drawing. Mine was "Esmeralda," about a pretty girl and a gun, with drawings of fish and the sea upon it, inscribed to "Lady Rue of New York." Steve got "Noodles," about a numbers runner from the twenties, and Emmett got "Bree Stewart,"" which was a brief history of Don's start on the island and his influence upon it.

Like most rebels, Don had a penchant for asking startling questions unrelated to immediate concerns. Houses of prostitution were a favorite subject, coming at us straight out of the blue, as was his editor, "AllBalls," who comes to stay at Habitat, his hotel, in return for her editing services. Apparently, this woman is a fearless rescue diver who once pulled a body up from 172 feet, hence the moniker. As he recounted the story of AllBalls, Emmett was in paroxysms of giggles. Being with Don was like going back to 1962. I could see the sort of place Bonaire had been when he'd arrived here, when young, and the world was not so weary and delicate.

I talked about how much fun we'd been having in the water, and how much I loved the reef, bracing myself to hear how much better it had been in times gone by. He did not disappoint. I heard about when the staghorn coral was so big and healthy that tips of it poked out of the water, and the reef grew in so dense at the shore that it was virtually impenetrable. In order to make a reef window, he and a team of divers had to sometimes dynamite paths through it, a practice that he regrets now.

Eventually the conversation came around to the environment. It was bound to. We spoke of how the pressures of global warming and the acidification of the oceans are hurting the reefs. He mentioned Hurricane Lenny in 1999, (one of Bonaire's few), having done quite a lot of damage, especially around Klein Bonaire. For Don, environmentalism began long ago, when he began to see the real-time effects of tourism upon his paradise. For example, a chunk of coral the size of your hand can take 20 years to grow. Science will tell you this, but only having a deep familiarity with the reef scape will make it real. After opening his reef windows, Don became radicalized by the sorts of abuses he witnessed. For a while, there was a run on black coral. When intact with stem and tree, it is probably the best-known shape of any coral. That is because so much of it has been extracted from the sea and made into living room ornaments and jewelry holders. On Google, I found many more pictures of black coral dead than alive. Don realized people were going out on dives with him and savaging the reefs for resale. He was horrified.

He wrote of having trouble sleeping, remembering the Governor's condition in '62, ". . . if my island is a better place because of you, then . . ." A tipping point was when one diver under his watch removed a pod of coral a foot square. Don dragged him to the surface and ordered him to put the coral back. It was the principle of the thing because, as he had briefed every diver, once broken from the main body, the coral would not survive.

The man still objected, and insisted on taking it. The shouting attracted a crowd on the beach to watch the showdown. Don, switching to his "instructor's voice," broadcast to them that "a crime was being committed," as the man had received an orientation at his dive shop that strictly forbade taking anything from the reef. There was a struggle and eventually the man unclenched his hand from the pod, where it drifted to the sea floor. One tourist taunted, "They paid for their vacation, didn't they?" Don said, with no small degree of emotion, "That piece they've destroyed shall never, NEVER be replaced in our lifetime." He was so furious that he took the man and his wife to the airport and personally put them on a plane.

From a self-described "reef rapist" (spear fishing, aquarium fish trapping), Don was becoming Bonaire's first environmentalist. Eventually, due to his influence, removing anything from the reef at all became a crime on Bonaire. Under the jurisdiction of the National Underwater Marine Park, the 25-mile-long reef has been protected from immediate theft and the divers who claim to love it since 1979. Captain Don's Habitat, Don's hotel dedicated to divers, opened in 1976. Environmentally forward looking, it was built with low impact construction, solar water heaters and a very successful waste water recycling system for gardens, of Don's design, that has been emulated throughout Bonaire. An ad hoc engineer, salvage mechanic, and carpenter, Don spent a lifetime developing the hotel strip, always with an awareness of the delicacy of marine resources. For Don, environmentalism is encapsulated on his island. At the time of our visit, the new Netherlands government had begun implementing a massive 35-million-dollar sewer project to control the effects of effluent on the reef.

Some believed that drilling down into an island made out of limestone rock would be as traumatic as the effluent. This was a matter for much debate. Despite his knighthood, Don complained that he was unable to get a hearing for his ideas with the power structure of the new Netherlands government. A businessperson himself, he felt at odds with the business and political climate on Bonaire. "The hotels all hate me," he said with some glee, even though he has a significant stake in Habitat.

If Don was still living in 1962, Janet was fully in the now. And if we were chimeras, arrived to Don's table from the future, then Janet was overseer to the present, long-time love, guide, and emissary of practicality, bringing the conversation back to the matter at hand.

I had brought my computer, unfortunately with a dead battery, so Janet ran an extension cord through window. I was fascinated to learn that Island Grower runs completely on solar. There was a glitch of some kind, but she got it running. Then

Emmett showed us his growing collection of Hermit crabs, and Janet got him a bucket for them. She asked him, "How did the shells they lived in get all the way from the sea to the interior of the island where we were?" Emmett didn't have an answer for that. I liked watching him ponder the question, though, before he trotted off with my camera to take pictures of the *kunuku*.

Looking at pictures of our house, specifically our absolutely bare trellis, Janet suggested what others had called "climbing yellow" or alamanda. The stuff is Bonaire's ivy, with waxy, medium, green leaves and cheerful, yellow blooms. Though very lush looking, it doesn't need a lot of water. For the front of the house, she consulted with Don, and he said seder trees. Everything in threes, or at least most things. Later they showed us seders about four feet high, with delicate pink blooms, and we put three onto the trolley.

Steve asked if we could try some bougainvillea. "Why not," said Janet. It was exciting to think that bougainvillea might thrive in our garden. I had seen it here and there on Bonaire but hardly dared to think such luxuries were possible. Janet explained that the roots are delicate but as long as planted out of the wind, and watered regularly, they had a good chance of taking hold.

I mentioned a tree I've seen around called a flamboyant, with intricate double pinnate leaves, and vermillion blossoms at this time of year. It is a Hobbit sort of tree, dwarfing some of the old sweet Bonairean cottages I've seen in Kralendijk and Antriol. In August, in bloom, it looks like it's on fire, hence the name. Also called a royal poinciana, Janet added, "That one will drop all its leaves in the driest months." It is a slow grower with a canopy shape, and a very pretty, twisted trunk, which might be as nice even without leaves, I later mused.

Like the most persuasive people, Don asked questions. He went from the map he had made. What was relationship of the house to the street and the sun? Where was the sea? From where did the trade winds come? All the while, he was formulating and sketching, Janet consulting with him from time to time. For a long time he had no suggestions. He wanted to know where the diabase had come from, but we couldn't say. He and Janet went over the possible sources and the pros and cons of each. We just hoped we had gotten the right stuff.

They showed us pictures of the drought-resistant gardens they had done at Habitat. There was a copious use of volcanic rock and sometimes boulders as decorative features that also hold in the soil. Don thought we should head in a similar direction in terms of design, and I guess because of all the space we had to fill. Janet went over each and every possibility—what the plants will need in terms of water and sun, how they might fare, and especially how big they would get. This of course was very important because these little striplings we'd be buying today would become, we hoped, monsters in the future, some getting there sooner than others. For instance, moringas and seders would grow fast but others, such as the calabash and buttonwoods, would take a long time.

Janet talked about the "hardscape" of the property. The hardscape is the design, everything that is concrete or gravel, including the driveway and paths. Would there be an addition later? A pagoda in back? A pool? Another porch? We would need to think about it all when positioning these trees. She made a really excellent suggestion, that hadn't occurred to us, which was to move the gate and the parking spot to the north corner of the property. Why, with so much land, have a car parked in front of the house? Plant out the front garden for privacy and to make a prettier view from inside. It was an invaluable idea that we later implemented when redoing the wall.

She said the best thing to do would be to look at everything they had at Island Grower. So we strolled along, Don in his wheelchair, Janet pausing here or there to explain something. Reduced sunlight drizzled through the shade cloth above rows and rows of plants. The whole place blended, one color into the next, varying shades of grey and earth, stone and brown, green and brighter green. Up ahead, Emmett collected more hermit crabs and yelled back at each iguana sighting. The iguanas skittered across the path in front of us or hung in the foliage, eyes shifting like small marbles. The heat, the sun, the arid quality, even the name, *kunuku*, reminded me of a trip to Africa when I was 12, where I met certain pioneering types, friends of my father, who preferred to live in "the bush" in open air compounds, with as little as possible between them and the wildlife on the plain.

We started piling the plants onto the trolley. The seders, three smooth bromeliads, three spiny bromeliads, five bougainvillea—white and scarlet and pink . . . Others were loaded on as we made our way through the compound, past the labyrinthine toolsheds, the cistern, the banana circle, and the new solar energy regulator they had just bought. Janet was very excited about this regulator, as the old one wasn't good at managing the current. She knew everything there is to know about solar, having been off the grid for decades. What better place for solar than Bonaire, I thought, where the sun shines almost every day? It made perfect sense, and I wondered why everyone wasn't on solar here.

Back at the house, Janet pointed out a tree that had done some damage to the roof the last time the wind was very high. She had wanted it taken down, because there were more branches threatening the porch. But Don had refused. As if to emphasize the point, he slowly shook his head, with nothing of the "showman" we had come to know. House be damned, that tree was not coming down. In its branches, there was a mockingbird nest, now dormant, ready for the next generation.

Don motioned with his chin to the trolley full of plants. "No irrigation, right?"

Yes, we had mentioned that we were pretty much broke, so no irrigation this year.

"We have it here. Have to. Gardener?" "Check."

"Who?"

"We're going to find one in the neighborhood. Frans has got someone." "Bring me a sample of that diabase," said Don.

"Okay."

"Make sure you fertilize."

"Okay." Emmett came up, looking frazzled again, his pockets bulging. "What happened?" I asked.

He pulled his pockets out. Four or five hermit crabs had taken up residence inside. Their claws sunk deep, they hung from the fabric like bibelots.

"Emmett!" I laughed. We all did. We could hardly believe it. He was lucky not to have a crab fused to his leg or worse.

"You know, you can take some home," said Janet, "and just set them off in your garden!"

At our urging, Emmett stripped off his shorts. Eventually the crabs unhinged themselves and were collected again in the bucket.

As we made our way toward the gate, I reflected that it's one thing to spend a few days or weeks in a setting like the *kunuku*, quite another to spend a lifetime. One has to really want a different kind of life and along with it comes a keen desire to let oneself be shaped by wilderness, more than by the society of people (whose culture arose out of *fending off* nature). So this goes against the grain. It's a unique way of seeing where value is in the world.

When I met Don, I could see that the mystique and culture of Bonaire extended more or less directly from him, and that in the early '60s, things could have gone in any direction. Bonaire could be all high rises and casinos now, though it is possible that the lack of beaches would have prevented it going the way of Aruba. But were we now on the tail end of the great wave? Did we just catch the last of the original idea of this place, God's idea, floating around, somewhat stale, in the web's permanent ether? Did we get sucked in by out-of-date "green" articles about the now-too-expensive-to-operate wind power plant?

There are many that think the new "more Dutch than before" government's policies will not safeguard the island's natural resources. There are many that think the unspoken, underlying policy of the new government is geared to short-term business prospects based in the Netherlands. There are many that think the local side of the government, mostly run by native Bonaireans, is intractably corrupt and all they want is to get the money out as fast as possible. I don't know. I just arrived, starry-eyed, on a raft of similar starry-eyed tourists so taken with the trade winds, the clucking, chattering birds, the hardscrabble quality, the undersea adventure and even the mud, that we just plunked our money down.

"Get a hose, you'll need that," said Don.

Then he wanted to make sure we had the right type of hose. Black rubber and 50 feet.

I wrote it all down in my notebook.

"Good thing you've got four spigots," he said.

And suddenly, I realized what Don was doing. He was making sure his plants were going to a good home.

Epilogue

April 2020

Don and Janet had the soil sample analyzed, and recommended salt-tolerant buttonwood trees as a privacy barrier to block out the apartment building. On that visit in 2012, we put in the first four buttonwoods from Island Grower, and I decided to name the house "Buttonwood Cottage." I wasn't sure why, I just liked the name. Over the years we added a cactus garden, a calabash, a flamboyant, more bougainvillea, two more sea grapes, three manila palms, two foxtail palms, two Spanish olives, and seven coconut palms, some from Island

Grower and also many from Greenlabel, the garden center in Kralendijk.

With the house outfitted and the garden launched, we were able to put it up for rent. At first we had some long-term renters at the low end, mainly students from the nearby marine biology center, where our neighbor Caren worked. As the garden filled in we began doing vacation rentals through Airbnb, which were more lucrative, none more than a month. Mostly one week. Americans, Dutch, English, Italians. Almost all divers. Some years we made a profit of five to ten thousand dollars. But when we'd arrive for our own vacation, there would be a lot of work. Painting, replacing things, things broken, etc. Over time, we were able to cut back by about 50 percent, renting only in the more profitable winter months, making enough to cover utilities and garden maintenance and taxes. We found our wonderful house manager, Sebastian "Baasje" Paluso, who has been with us now for six years. In terms of investment, I'd say the house will be profitable to sell after a long period of time. But profit was never the main objective.

To our surprise, the original four buttonwood trees from Island Grower did so well that their trunks are now six to seven inches thick. On each visit back to Bonaire, we planted a few more, including three silver buttonwoods, and now the entire plot is ringed with them. Every time we come in from New York, the trees are fuller and the palms are taller, rustling in the trade winds as I had envisioned. A guava seed "volunteered" in one of the pots, and the gardeners replanted it where I can see it from the kitchen window. It is doing well and might even bear fruit, they said. In 2015, we put in a cactus garden in front of the house, ringed with volcanic rock, as Don had suggested. In 2017, we hired Hans Rietveld again to construct a big *palapa*, (straw hut) in the back garden, behind the kitchen. This is where I spend most of my time when visiting. It is a wonderful spot to meditate in the mornings, the birds coming to life, and mourning doves strutting by, sipping from the irrigation. Friends come down to visit and love it as much as we do, swimming, windsurfing, diving, and snorkeling, living mostly outside and relaxing in those lovely trade winds. The restaurants have improved. Bonaire has grown by quite a lot, but still, per the restrictions, there are no high-rise hotels. There are forces trying to develop Bonaire, and equally strong forces trying to put the brakes on. Kaya India feels much the same as it did when we bought it. A new building went up on the corner. Yvonne Domacasse is still on her porch in the mornings, and sometimes in the evenings, keeping an eye on everything. One time our irrigation timer broke, soaking the garden, and she called our house manager, Baasje. Another time a renter left the gates open, and donkeys (unwanted now!) got in and ate three manila palms. Again, she called Baasje to come and manage the situation.

Sometimes the dogs are loud (none as bad as Bollocks), and we just put up with it. As for the crime problem, we have had two incidents in eight years. The first was a slightly bent doorframe where kids tried to get in with a crow bar. The second—these would have had to have been adults—clipped the padlock on the steel enclosure on the porch and made off with the washing machine. We thought it was the moustache-twirling builder from Venezuela, who lived nearby, and had unsuccessfully tried to fleece us at the end of the job. Had he waited for his moment all those years, and struck? It was hard to believe, but we refused to let it ruin Bonaire for us. A while ago, a neighbor's flock of chickens went wild, and they were all over the place, roosters crowing at four in the morning . . . a terrible nuisance. But they know to stay off of our plot now, because, once when visiting, I picked up the habit of throwing rock missiles at them. It worked! In my house notes for the vacation rental, I recommend that the renters do too. The kids love it! That's true country living. Not scrubbed and perfect, but full of funny stories.

In 2014, after a lifetime of diving adventures, Captain Don died at the age of 88. His hotel, Habitat, is still there on the hotel strip. On the lovely big porch overlooking the sea, Janet gives talks about their early years on Bonaire—how he came to be such an impassioned environmentalist and became the founder of Bonaire's National Underwater Marine Park. Though many have urged her to leave their *kunuku* and relocate closer to the town, I don't think she ever will. Every time we visit, she comes to Kaya India for a BBQ. She loves to see the progress of the garden that she and Don helped us design. It pleases her to see the plants and trees booming along, and that our original vision of what the house could be has been realized. Yvonne always comes for tea with one or another of her many grandchildren. I bring her things she wants from the States, notating in my Bonaire file titled "next time." We talk about the garden. She schools me in the local dialect, translating all of the plant names to Papiamento. In 2015 Frans and Caren pulled up stakes and went back to Caren's native Austin, Texas. A few years later they were living on Bonaire again, in a different neighborhood with their two daughters.

FarrarFiles

Made in the USA
Coppell, TX
18 June 2022